PRE-ISLAMIC ARCHAEOLOGY OF KUWAIT, NORTHEASTERN ARABIA, BAHRAIN, QATAR, UNITED ARAB EMIRATES AND OMAN: A BIBLIOGRAPHY

FIRST SUPPLEMENT
(1985-1995)

PRE-ISLAMIC ARCHAEOLOGY OF KUWAIT, NORTHEASTERN ARABIA, BAHRAIN, QATAR, UNITED ARAB EMIRATES AND OMAN: A BIBLIOGRAPHY

FIRST SUPPLEMENT (1985-1995)

by

K.G. STEVENS & E. HAERINCK

Vakgebied "Archeologie en kunstgeschiedenis van het Nabije Oosten"
Vakgroep "Talen en culturen van het Nabije Oosten en Noord-Afrika"
Universiteit Gent (Belgium)

PEETERS
LEUVEN

1996

ISBN 90-6831-865-9
D. 1996/0602/89

CONTENTS

GENERAL WORKS

PREHISTORY — 4TH MILLENNIUM B.C.

LATE 4TH MILLENNIUM — END 2ND MILLENNIUM B.C.

LATE 2ND MILLENNIUM B.C. — 7TH CENTURY A.D.

GENERAL WORKS

Bibliographies

603 E. HAERINCK & K.G. STEVENS, Pre-Islamic Archaeology of Kuwait, Northeastern Arabia, Bahrain, Qatar, United Arab Emirates and Oman: A Bibliography, Gent, 1985, xii + 53 p., 1 map.

604 ANONYMUS, Bibliography, *in* Bahrain through the ages, the Archaeology (Shaikha Haya Ali al-Khalifa & M. Rice, eds.), London, 1986, pp. 497-516.

605 Y. CALVET & J.-F. SALLES, Bibliographical notes (1984-1988), *in* Failaka. Fouilles françaises 1986-1988 (Y. Calvet & J. Gachet, eds.) [= Travaux de la Maison de l'Orient 18], Lyon, 1990, pp. 11-22, 1 fig.

Congresses, symposia and newsletters

606 ANONYMUS, The Seminar for Arabian Studies. A Summary of its meetings since 1968, *in* Proceedings of the Seminar for Arabian Studies 15 [= Proceedings of the 18th Seminar for Arabian Studies 1984], 1985, pp. 99-109.

607 Newsletters of The Society for Arabian Studies, London, 1989-1995: n°. 1 (December 1989) 7 p.; n°. 2 (December 1990) 7 p.; n°. 3 (March 1992) 10 p.; n°. 4 (February 1993) 20 p.; n°. 5 (March 1994) 24 p.; n°. 6 (March 1995) 28 p.

608 S. SEARIGHT, The Society for Arabian Studies, *in* Arts & The Islamic World 25 [= Special Volume: Saudi Arabia. Architecture, Archaeology and the Arts], 1994, pp. 86-87.

General studies on archaeology, different countries and/or periods

609 H. von WISSMANN, Arabien, [= Dokumente zur Entdeckungsgeschichte I], Stuttgart, 1965, 366 p., 1 Pl.

610 I. SHAHID, Pre-Islamic Arabia, *in* The Cambridge History of Islam, Vol. I: The Central Islamic Lands (P.M. Holt, A.K.S. Lambton & B. Lewis, eds.), Cambridge, 1970, pp. 3-29 & 736-739, 1 map.

611 H. von WISSMANN, Über die frühe Geschichte Arabiens und das Entstehen des Sabäerreiches. Die Geschichte von Saba' 1, Wien, 1975, 112 p., 18 Abb. (esp. pp. 5-26).

612 B. DOE, Monuments of South Arabia, [= Arabia past and present series 12], Naples, Cambridge & New York, 1983, vi + 284 p., 83 fig., 32 Pl., 8 maps.

613 G. BIBBY, Looking for Dilmun. The Search for a lost Civilization. (With a new Preface 16 April 1984), [= Penguin Travel Library], Harmondsworth, 1984, 410 p., fig., 32 Pl. [cfr. Bibliography n°. 15].

614 P.J. PARR, The Present State of Archaeological Research in the Arabian Peninsula: Achievements of the Past, and Problems for the Future, *in* Pre-Islamic Arabia. Studies in the History of Arabia II [= Proceedings of the Second International Symposium on Studies in the History of Arabia 1399/1979], Riyadh, 1984, pp. 43-54.

615 S. CLEUZIOU, Une région découvre son passé: le Golfe, *in* Le Proche-Orient ancien. Le Grand Atlas de l'Archéologie [= Encyclopaedia Universalis], Paris, 1985, pp. 186-187, 7 fig.

616 S. CLEUZIOU, Golfe (pays du): Archéologie, *in* Le Grand Atlas de l'Archéologie [= Encyclopaedia Universalis], Paris, 1985, pp. 560-568, ill.

617 L. COSTANTINI, Considerazioni su alcuni reperti di palma da dattero e sul centro di origine e l'area di coltivazione della phoenix dactylifera, *in* Orientalia Iosephi Tucci Memoriae Dicata (G. Gnoli & L. Lancioti, eds.), Roma, 1985, pp. 209-217.

618 M. RICE, Search for the paradise land. An introduction to the archaeology of Bahrain and the Arabian Gulf, from the earliest times to the death of Alexander the Great, London & New York, 1985, vi + 298 p., var. ill., XVI Pl.

619 A. ROUGEULLE, Date "incubators" in Bahrain and Oman: The problem of the emergence of date processing techniques, *in* Dilmun 13, 1985-'86, pp. 34-46, 3 fig.

620 M. TOSI, Early maritime cultures of the Arabian Gulf and the Indian Ocean, *in* Bahrain through the ages, the Archaeology (Shaikha Haya Ali al-Khalifa & M. Rice, eds.), London, 1986, pp. 94-107, fig. 23-24.

621 M. TOSI, The Emerging Picture of Prehistoric Arabia, *in* Annual Review of Anthropology 15, 1986, pp. 461-490, 1 map.

622 S. CLEUZIOU, Les pays du Golfe il y a 5000 ans, *in* Dossiers Histoire et Archéologie 122 [= De l'Euphrate à l'Indus. Les plus anciennes civilisations], 1987, pp. 46-47, 3 ill.

623 R. DALONGEVILLE & P. SANLAVILLE, Confrontation des datations isotopiques avec les données géomorphologiques et archéologiques à propos des variations relatives du niveau marin sur la rive arabe du Golfe Persique,

in Chronologies du Proche Orient/Chronologies in the Near East. Relative Chronologies and Absolute Chronology 16000–4000 B.P., C.N.R.S. International Symposium, Lyon (France) 24–28 November 1986 (O. Aurenche, J. Evin & F. Hours, eds.) [= BAR (British Archaeological Reports) International Series 379/II], Oxford, 1987, pp. 567-588, 9 fig.

624 T. HOWARD-CARTER, Dilmun: At Sea or not at Sea? — A Review Article, *in* Journal of Cuneiform Studies 39, 1987, pp. 54-117.

625 J.-F. SALLES, Le Golfe Arabo-Persique, *in* Dossiers Histoire et Archéologie 122 [= De l'Euphrate à l'Indus. Les plus anciennes civilisations], 1987, pp. 48-50, 7 ill.

626 P. SANLAVILLE, R. DALONGEVILLE, J. EVIN & R. PASKOFF, Modifications du tracé littoral sur la côte arabe du Golfe Persique en relation avec l'archéologie, *in* M. Euzenat & R. Paskoff, Déplacements des lignes de rivage en Méditerranée d'après les données de l'archéologie. Colloques internationaux C.N.R.S. (P. Trousset, ed.), Paris, 1987, pp. 211-222, 6 fig.

627 M.A. KONISHI, T. GOTOH & Y. AKASHI, Archaeological Researches in the Gulf — A Preliminary Report of the Excavations in Bahrain and Qatar, 1987/8 Season, *in* Orient XXIV, 1988, pp. 18-46, fig. 1-7, Pl. 1-6.

628 M.A. KONISHI, T. GOTOH & Y. AKASHI, Excavations in Bahrain and Qatar 1987/8 Season, Gulf Archaeological Projects Report I, Center for Asian Area Studies [= Occasional Papers 3], Tokyo, 1989, 22 p., 28 Pl.

629 H.-P. UERPMANN, Problems of archaeo-zoological research in Eastern Arabia, *in* Oman Studies, Papers on the archaeology and history of Oman [= Serie Orientale Roma 63 (P.M. Costa & M. Tosi, eds.)], Roma, 1989, pp. 163-168.

630 J. BESANÇON, R. DALONGEVILLE & P. SANLAVILLE, Le piémont occidental de la montagne d'Oman, *in* Méditerranée, revue géographique des pays méditerranéens, n°. hors série [= 3e Forum national de géomorphologie, Aix-en-Provence, 26–27 Septembre 1990, Genèse et évolution des Pie(d)monts], 1990, pp. 12-14, 1 fig.

631 R.N. FRYE, The "Persian Gulf" and Changes in Nomenclature, *in* Jerusalem Studies in Arabic and Islam 13, 1990, pp. 33-43.

632 D.T. POTTS, The Arabian Gulf in Antiquity I. From Prehistory to the Fall of the Achaemenian Empire, Oxford, 1990, xxvii + 419 p., 1 map, 44 fig., 8 Tab., XII Pl.

633 J. ZARINS, Obsidian and the Red Sea Trade. Prehistoric Aspects, *in* South Asian Archaeology 1987 [= Proceedings of the Ninth International Conference of the Association of South Asian Archaeologists in Western Europe held in the Fondazione Giorgio Cini, Venice (M. Taddei, ed.)], Rome, 1990, pp. 507-541, 7 fig., 2 Tab.

634 J.F. HEALEY, Ugarit and Arabia: a balance sheet, *in* Proceedings of the Seminar for Arabian Studies 21 [= Proceedings of the 24th Seminar for Arabian Studies, held at Oxford on 24–26th July 1990], 1991, pp. 69-78.

635 H.-P. UERPMANN, Equus africanus in Arabia, *in* Equids in the Ancient World (R.H Meadow & H.-P. Uerpmann, eds.) [= Beihefte zum Tübinger Atlas des Vorderen Orients, Reihe A (Naturwissenschaften) 19/2], Wiesbaden, 1991, pp. 12-33, 8 fig., 7 Tab.

636 R. DALONGEVILLE, V. DE MEDWECKI & P. SANLAVILLE, Evolution du Piémont occidental de l'Oman depuis le Pléistocène supérieur, *in* Déserts, Présent, Futur [= Actes du 116e Congrès National des Sociétés Savantes, Chambéry, 29–30 avril 1991, Section des Sciences], Paris, 1992, pp. 97-109, 4 fig., 1 Tab.

637 B.E. DENTON & H.I. MACADAM, The other Mediterranean: Archaeology and the Gulf, *in* Journal of Interdisciplinary History 23, 1992, pp. 119-131.

638 B. GRONEBERG, Le golfe arabo-persique, vu depuis Mari, *in* Florilegium marianum. Receuil d'études en l'honneur de Michel Fleury (J.-M. Durand, ed.), [= Supplément à N.A.B.U. n°. 1], Paris, 1992, pp. 69-80.

639 P. LOMBARD, Review of "D.T. Potts: The Arabian Gulf in Antiquity, Vol. I. From Prehistory to the Fall of the Achaemenian Empire, Oxford, 1990", *in* Topoi 2, 1992, pp. 195-199.

640 D.T. POTTS, The Chronology of the Archaeological Assemblages from the Head of the Arabian Gulf to the Arabian Sea, 8000–1750 B.C., *in* Chronologies in Old World Archaeology [= Third Edition (R.W. Ehrich, ed.)], Chicago & London, 1992, Vol. I: pp. 63-76, Vol. II: pp. 77-89, 4 fig., 1 Tab.

641 P. SANLAVILLE, Changements climatiques dans la péninsule arabique durant le Pléistocène supérieur et l'Holocène, *in* Paléorient 18/1, 1992, pp. 5-26, 11 fig.

642 J. ZARINS, Archaeological and Chronological Problems within the Greater Southwest Asian Arid Zone: 8500–1850 BC, *in* Chronologies in Old World Archaeology, [= Third Edition (R.W. Ehrich, ed.)], Chicago & London, 1992, Vol. I: pp. 42-62, Vol. II: pp. 61-76.

643 R. DALONGEVILLE, P. BERNIER, B. DUPUIS & V. DE MEDWECKI, Les variations récentes de la ligne de rivage dans le Golfe Persique: L'exemple de la lagune d'Umm al-Qowayn (Emirats Arabes Unis), *in* Bulletin de l'Institut Géologique. Bassin d'Aquitaine n°. 53, Bordeaux, 1993, pp. 179-192, 6 fig.

644 D.T. POTTS, The Late Prehistoric, Protohistoric, and Early Historic Periods in Eastern Arabia (ca. 5000–1200 B.C.), *in* Journal of World Prehistory 7/2, 1993, pp. 163-212, 11 fig.

645 P. SANLAVILLE, J. BESANÇON, R. BOUCHARLAT, R. DALONGEVILLE, J. EVIN, B. GEYER, J.-L. HUOT, P. LOMBARD, J. MARGUERON, V. DE MEDWECKI & J.-F. SALLES, Occupation humaine et environnement en Mésopotamie et sur la rive arabe du Golfe Persique depuis le Néolithique, *in* Pour une histoire de l'environment [= Actes du programme scientifique et du colloque de mars 1991 sur l'histoire de l'environnement et des phénomènes naturels (C. Beck & R. Delort, eds.)], CNRS Editions, Paris, 1993, pp. 21-41, 6 fig.

646 F. HOURS, O. AURENCHE, J. CAUVIN, M.-C. CAUVIN, L. COPELAND & P. SANLAVILLE avec la collaboration de P. LOMBARD, Atlas des sites du Proche Orient (14000–5700 B.P.) [= Travaux de la Maison de l'Orient Méditerranéen 24], Lyon, 1994, 522 p., maps (see list of sites: Saudi Arabia, p. 475; Bahrain, p. 475; Koweit, p. 489 & Qatar, pp. 490-491).

647 K.A. KITCHEN, Documentation for Ancient Arabia. Part I: Chronological Framework and Historical Sources [= World of Ancient Arabia series 1], Liverpool, 1994, 268 p., Tab. A-Y, 2 fig.

648 S. MERY, La céramique, témoin de la dynamique culturelle en Arabie durant la Protohistoire, *in* Terre cuite et Société. La céramique: document technique, économique et culturel, Juan-les-Pins, 1994, pp. 363-380.

649 P.R.S. MOOREY, Ancient Mesopotamian Materials and Industries. The Archaeological Evidence, Oxford, 1994, 414 p., 24 fig.

650 D.T. POTTS, Contributions to the agrarian history of Eastern Arabia I. Implements and cultivation techniques, *in* Arabian archaeology and epigraphy 5/3, 1994, pp. 158-168, 6 fig.

651 D.T. POTTS, Contributions to the agrarian history of Eastern Arabia II. The cultivars, *in* Arabian archaeology and epigraphy 5/4, 1994, pp. 236-275, 13 Tab.

652 M. RICE, The Archaeology of the Arabian Gulf c. 5000–323 BC, [= The Experience of Archaeology (A. Wheatcroft, ed.)], London & New York, 1994, 369 p., 9 fig., 5 maps.

653 M. RICE, The Arabian Peninsula and the Recovery of the Past, *in* Arts & The Islamic World 25 [= Special Volume: Saudi Arabia. Architecture, Archaeology and the Arts], 1994, pp. 56-71, ill.

654 J.-F. SALLES, India and the Near East: The Bridge of Arabia, *in* Journal of the Asiatic Society of Bangladesh, Humanities 39/1, 1994, pp. 41-58.

Kuwait

655 S. PATITUCCI & G. UGGERI, Failakah. Insediamenti medievali islamici. Ricerche e scavi nel Kuwait [= La Fenice 4], Roma, 1984, xvi + 458 p., 106 fig., CVI Pl., 8 Tab.

656 Y. Calvet, A. Caubet & J.-F. Salles, French Excavations at Failaka, 1984, *in* Proceedings of the Seminar for Arabian Studies 15 [= Proceedings of the 18th Seminar for Arabian Studies 1984], 1985, pp. 11-26, 7 fig.

657 J.-F. Salles, Failaka, une île des dieux au large de Koweit, *in* Comptes rendus des séances de l'annéé 1985 de l'Academie des Inscriptions et Belles-Lettres, Paris, novembre-décembre 1985, pp. 572-593, 12 fig.

658 Y. Calvet & J.-F. Salles, Avant-propos — Foreword, *in* Failaka. Fouilles Françaises 1984-1985 (Y. Calvet & J.-F. Salles, eds.) [= Travaux de la Maison de l'Orient 12], Lyon, 1986, pp. 7-12, fig. 1-3.

659 J.-F. Salles, Les fouilles de Tell Khazneh — Excavations at Tell Khazneh, *in* Failaka. Fouilles Françaises 1984-1985 (Y. Calvet & J.-F. Salles, eds.) [= Travaux de la Maison de l'Orient 12], Lyon, 1986, pp. 107-142, fig. 46-58.

660 F. al-Wohaibi, Survey of Umm an-Namel Island, State of Kuwait, Indiana, 1987, 378 p. [= Dissertation Abstracts International. Section A. Humanities and Social Sciences, U.S.A. 48, n°. 5, 1987, pp. 1241-1242].

661 D.T. Potts, Review of J.-F. Salles e.a., Failaka Fouilles Françaises 1983 and Y. Calvet & J.-F. Salles e.a., Failaka Fouilles Françaises 1984-1985, *in* Archiv für Orientforschung XXXV, 1988, pp. 219-222.

662 J.-F. Salles, Review of S. Patitucci & G. Uggeri: Failakah. Insediamenti medievali islamici. Ricerche e scavi nel Kuwait [= La Fenice 4], Roma, *in* Syria LXV/1-2, 1988, pp. 253-258.

663 A. Salle, Koweit: archéologie et histoire, *in* Archéologia 252, 1989, pp. 14-15, 5 fig.

664 J.-F. Salles, Failaka. Berceau d'une mémoire, *in* Koweiti [= Catalogue d'exposition — L'Institut du Monde Arabe], Paris, 1989, pp. 9-14, 2 Pl.

665 J.-F. Salles & O. Salles, Koweit, Paris, 1989, 273 p., ill.

666 J. Cataliotti-Valdina, Les coquillages de Failaka, *in* Failaka. Fouilles françaises 1986-1988 (Y. Calvet & J. Gachet, eds.) [= Travaux de la Maison de l'Orient 18], Lyon, 1990, pp. 71-84, 1 fig., 16 Tabl., III Pl.

667 R. Dalongeville, Présentation physique générale de l'île de Failaka, *in* Failaka. Fouilles françaises 1986-1988 (Y. Calvet & J. Gachet, eds.) [= Travaux de la Maison de l'Orient 18], Lyon, 1990, pp. 23-40, 13 fig.

668 H. David, La vaisselle en chlorite de Failaka, *in* Failaka. Fouilles françaises 1986-1988 (Y. Calvet & J. Gachet, eds.) [= Travaux de la Maison de l'Orient 18], Lyon, 1990, pp. 141-147, 20 fig.

669 J. Desse & N. Desse-Berset, La faune: les mammifères et les poissons, *in* Failaka. Fouilles françaises 1986-1988 (Y. Calvet & J. Gachet, eds.) [= Travaux de la Maison de l'Orient 18], Lyon, 1990, pp. 51-70, 24 fig.

670 J.-F. SALLES, Avant-propos (Foreword), *in* Failaka. Fouilles françaises 1986-1988 (Y. Calvet & J. Gachet, eds.) [= Travaux de la Maison de l'Orient 18], Lyon, 1990, pp. 7-10.

671 G. WILLCOX, The plant remains from Hellenistic and Bronze Age levels at Failaka, Kuwait. A preliminary report, *in* Failaka. Fouilles françaises 1986-1988 (Y. Calvet & J. Gachet, eds.) [= Travaux de la Maison de l'Orient 18], Lyon, 1990, pp. 43-50, 1 fig.

672 G. SEERY, Early settlers, *in* Kuwait, *in* Arabian Profiles. The Arab Gulf Cooperation Council (AGCC) — Bahrain, Kuwait, Oman, Qatar, Saudi Arabia & UAE (I. Fairservice & C. Grieve, eds.), Dubai, 1991, pp. 48-49, 1 fig.

673 P. VINE & P. CASEY, Kuwait. A Nation's Story, London, 1992, 163 p., ill.

Northeastern Arabia

674 ANONYMUS, The Eastern Region: Hasa and Qatif Oases, *in* An Introduction to Saudi Arabian Antiquities, Dept. of Antiquities and Museums, Ministry of Education, Riyath, 1975, pp. 129-156, 1 map, 41 Pl.

675 G. BURKHOLDER, An Arabian Collection. Artifacts from the Eastern Province, Boulder City, 1984, viii + 224 p., 67 fig., 6 maps.

676 D.T. POTTS, Miscellanea Hasaitica [= Carsten Niebuhr Institute Publications 9], Copenhagen, 1989, 95 p., 130 fig.

677 M.A. NAYEEM, Saudi Arabia [= Prehistory and Protohistory of the Arabian Peninsula I], Hyderabad, 1990, 280 p., 10 maps, 4 Tab., 2 charts, 97 fig., XXXX fig., XVI Pl.

678 B. BRENTJES, Südturkmenien und Ostarabien, *in* Golf–Archäologie. Mesopotamien, Iran, Kuwait, Bahrain, Vereinigte Arabische Emirate und Oman (K. Schippmann, A. Herling & J.-F. Salles, eds.) [= Internationale Archäologie 6, Buch am Erlbach], Göttingen & Lyon, 1991, pp. 113-120, 6 Abb.

679 A.R.T. al-ANSARY, Pre-Islamic Antiquities in Saudi Arabia, *in* Arts & The Islamic World 25 [= Special Volume: Saudi Arabia. Architecture, Archaeology and the Arts], 1994, pp. 37-39 & 48.

680 G.R.D. KING, The Development of Archaeology in Saudi Arabia, *in* Arts & The Islamic World 25 [= Special Volume: Saudi Arabia. Architecture, Archaeology and the Arts], 1994, pp. 49-55.

681 A.H. MASRY, The Historic Legacy of Saudi Arabia, *in* Arts & The Islamic World 25 [= Special Volume: Saudi Arabia. Architecture, Archaeology and the Arts], 1994, pp. 44-48.

682 A.H. MASRY, Archaeology and the Establishment of Museums in Saudi Arabia, *in* Museums and the Making of "Ourselves". The Role of Objects in National Identity (F.E.S. Kaplan, ed.), London, 1994, pp. 125-167, 11 fig.

683 ANONYMUS, The Museum of Archaeology and Ethnography, Riyath, Saudi Arabia. A Handbook for Visitors, Department of Antiquities & Museums, Ministry of Education, Riyath, s.d., 48 p.

Bahrain

684 D.T. POTTS, Reflections on the history and archaeology of Bahrain, *in* Journal of the American Oriental Society 105/4, 1985, pp. 675-710, 8 Tab.

685 A.L. KANOO, Names of Bahrain through the Ages: Dilmun — Tylos — Awal — Bahrain [= Summary of the Arabic text], *in* Dilmun 13, 1985-'86, p. 61.

686 A.R. MOSAMEH, Bahrain Museum Experience, *in* Dilmun 13, 1985-'86, pp. 28-33.

687 A.R. MOSAMEH, Bahrain through the Ages [= Summary of the Arabic Text], *in* Dilmun 13, 1985-'86, p. 63.

688 B.M. FEILDEN, The presentation and conservation of archaeological sites in Bahrain, *in* Bahrain through the ages, the Archaeology (Shaikha Haya Ali al-Khalifa & M. Rice, eds.), London, 1986, pp. 470-479, fig. 162-165.

689 K. HØJGAARD, Dental anthropological investigations on Bahrain, *in* Bahrain through the ages, the Archaeology (Shaikha Haya Ali al-Khalifa & M. Rice, eds.), London, 1986, pp. 64-71, fig. 19-20, 2 Tab.

690 C.E. LARSEN, Variation in holocene land use patterns on the Bahrain Islands: construction of a land use model, *in* Bahrain through the ages, the Archaeology (Shaikha Haya Ali al-Khalifa & M. Rice, eds.), London, 1986, pp. 25-46, fig. 6-11, 2 Tab.

691 P. SANLAVILLE & R. PASKOFF, Shoreline changes in Bahrain since the beginning of human occupation, *in* Bahrain through the ages, the Archaeology (Shaikha Haya Ali al-Khalifa & M. Rice, eds.), London, 1986, pp. 15-24, fig. 1-5.

692 M. KERVRAN, Qal'at al-Bahrain: cinq mille ans d'histoire, *in* Le Golfe à l'époque islamique, *in* Dossiers Histoire et Archéologie 122 [= De l'Euphrate à l'Indus. Les plus anciennes civilisations], 1987, pp. 51-52, 4 fig.

693 P. VINE, Pearls in Arabian Waters. The Heritage of Bahrain, 1987, 160 p., ill.

694 B. FROHLICH, M. KERVRAN, V. CARUSO & K. MCCORMICK, Noncontacting Terrain Conductivity Measurements at Qala'at al-Bahrain, *in* Dilmun 14, 1987-'88, pp. 74-89, 11 fig.

695 G. RIZZI, Mortars: A problem of Archaeology and Architectural conservation in Bahrain, *in* Dilmun 14, 1987-'88, pp. 51-60.

696 J.-F. SALLES, Review of "C.E. Larsen: Life and Land Use on the Bahrain Islands. The Geoarchaeology of an Ancient Society", *in* Bulletin of the American Schools of Oriental Research 271, 1988, pp. 79-82.

697 B. ANDRE, The Written Documents (Early Dilmun period to Tylos period), *in* Bahrain National Museum. Archaeological Collections I. A Selection of Pre-Islamic Antiquities from Excavations 1954-1975 (P. Lombard & M. Kervran, eds.), Manama, 1989, pp. 165-175, fig. 314-321.

698 D. BEYER, The Bahrain Seals (Early Dilmun period to Tylos period), *in* Bahrain National Museum. Archaeological Collections I. A Selection of Pre-Islamic Antiquities from Excavations 1954-1975 (P. Lombard & M. Kervran, eds.), Manama, 1989, pp. 133-164, fig. 242-313, 1 Tab.

699 S. KAY, Bahrain. Island Heritage, Dubai, 1989, 115 p., var. ill.

700 J.H. LITTLETON & B. FROHLICH, An Analysis of Dental Pathology and Diet on Historic Bahrain, *in* Paléorient 15/2, 1989, pp. 59-75, 1 fig., II Pl., 15 Tab.

701 H.I. MACADAM, Dilmun revisited (Review of Bahrain through the Ages: the Archaeology), *in* Arabian archaeology and epigraphy 1/2-3, 1990, pp. 49-87.

702 S. KAY, An ancient past, *in* Bahrain, *in* Arabian Profiles. The Arab Gulf Cooperation Council (AGCC) — Bahrain, Kuwait, Oman, Qatar, Saudi Arabia & UAE (I. Fairservice & C. Grieve, eds.), Dubai, 1991, pp. 18-20, 2 fig.

703 M.J. al-ANSARY, Cultural contacts and activities in Bahrain through the Ages, *in* Dilmun 15, 1991-'92, pp. 11-12.

704 K.E. RAJAB, Tree of Dilmun, *in* Dilmun 15, 1991-'92, pp. 67-72.

705 M.A. NAYEEM, Bahrain [= Prehistory and Protohistory of the Arabian Peninsula II], Hyderabad, 1992, 443 p., var. fig.

706 P. LOMBARD, Compte rendu d'une communication sur l'archéologie des deux mers: travaux récents à Bahrein, *in* Journal Asiatique 281-3/4, 1993, pp. 426-427.

707 P. VINE et alii, Bahrain National Museum (P. Vine, ed.), Bahrain & London, 1993, X + 177 p., var. fig., ill. & Pl.

708 J. CATALIOTTI-VALDINA, Les Coquillages, *in* F. Højlund & H.H. Andersen, Qala'at al-Bahrain, Vol. 1, The Northern City Wall and the Islamic Fortress. The Carlsberg Foundation's Gulf Project (P. Mortensen, ed.)

[= Jutland Archaeological Society Publications XXX:1], Aarhus, 1994, pp. 455-458, fig. 2096, 2 Annexes.

709 F. HØJLUND & H.H. ANDERSEN, Qala'at al-Bahrain, Vol. 1, The Northern City Wall and the Islamic Fortress. The Carlsberg Foundation's Gulf Project (P. Mortensen, ed.) [= Jutland Archaeological Society Publications XXX:1], Aarhus, 1994, 511 p., 2105 fig., III Tab., sections A-X & plans 1-11.

710 G. WILLCOX, Archaeobotanical finds, *in* F. Højlund & H.H. Andersen, Qala'at al-Bahrain, Vol. 1, The Northern City Wall and the Islamic Fortress. The Carlsberg Foundation's Gulf Project (P. Mortensen, ed.) [= Jutland Archaeological Society Publications XXX:1], Aarhus, 1994, pp. 459-462, fig. 2097-2103, IV Tab.

Qatar

711 B. NICHOLLS, Cultural treasury, *in* Qatar, *in* Arabian Profiles. The Arab Gulf Cooperation Council (AGCC) — Bahrain, Kuwait, Oman, Qatar, Saudi Arabia & UAE (I. Fairservice & C. Grieve, eds.), Dubai, 1991, pp. 104-107, 5 fig.

712 P. VINE & P. CASEY, The Heritage of Qatar, London, 1992, 159 p., var. ill.

United Arab Emirates

713 W.Y. al-TIKRITI, Archaeology in the UAE — The Fourth and Third Millenia BC, *in* Emirates Natural History Group (Abu Dhabi) Bulletin 20, July 1983, pp. 13-15.

714 S. KAY, Emirates Archaeological Heritage, Dubai, 1986, 82 p., var. ill., maps.

715 D. WHITE-COOPER, Rock Engravings in the U.A.E. and Musandam Peninsula, *in* Emirates Natural History Group (Abu Dhabi) Bulletin 31, March 1987, pp. 26-28, 12 fig.

716 S. KAY, Land of the Emirates and Archaeological Heritage, [= revised and combined reprint of "The Land of the Emirates" and "Emirates Archaeological Heritage"], Dubai, 1989, 107 p., var. fig., maps.

717 P. VINE & P. CASEY, Arab Gold. Heritage of the United Arab Emirates, London, 1989, 160 p., ill.

718 P. HELLYER, Retracing the past, *in* United Arab Emirates, *in* Arabian Profiles. The Arab Gulf Cooperation Council (AGCC) — Bahrain, Kuwait, Oman, Qatar, Saudi Arabia & UAE (I. Fairservice & C. Grieve, eds.), Dubai, 1991, pp. 141-143, 4 fig.

719 P. HELLYER, Recorders' Reports for 1990. Archaeology, *in* Tribulus. Bulletin of the Emirates Natural History Group 1/1, 1991, p. 28.

720 P. HELLYER, Recorders' Reports for January-June 1991. Archaeology and Palaeontology, *in* Tribulus. Bulletin of the Emirates Natural History Group 1/2, 1991, p. 31.

721 P. HELLYER, Recorders' Reports for July-December 1991. Archaeology and Palaeontology, *in* Tribulus. Bulletin of the Emirates Natural History Group 2/1, 1992, p. 27.

722 P. HELLYER, Recorders' Reports for January-June 1992. Archaeology and Palaeontology, *in* Tribulus. Bulletin of the Emirates Natural History Group 2/2, 1992, p. 41.

723 P. VINE & P. CASEY, United Arab Emirates. Heritage & Modern Development, London, 1992, 160 p., ill.

724 P. HELLYER, The UAE: A New Frontier in Archaeology, *in* Arts & The Islamic World 23 [= Special issue: Architecture, Archaeology and the Arts in the United Arab Emirates], 1993, pp. 41-44, 7 fig.

725 P. HELLYER, Recorders' Reports for July-December 1992. Archaeology and Palaeontology, *in* Tribulus. Bulletin of the Emirates Natural History Group 3/1, 1993, p. 27.

726 P. HELLYER, Recorders' Reports for January-June 1993. Archaeology and Palaeontology, *in* Tribulus. Bulletin of the Emirates Natural History Group 3/2, 1993, p. 21.

727 W.Y. al-TIKRITI, Al Ain Museum: Archaeology in the UAE since 1950's, *in* Arts & The Islamic World 23 [= Special issue: Architecture, Archaeology and the Arts in the United Arab Emirates], 1993, pp. 53-55, 2 fig.

728 P. HELLYER, Recorders' Reports. Archaeology and Palaeontology, *in* Tribulus. Bulletin of the Emirates Natural History Group 4/1, 1994, p. 25.

729 P. HELLYER, Recorders' Reports. Archaeology and Palaeontology, *in* Tribulus. Bulletin of the Emirates Natural History Group 4/2, 1994, p. 26.

730 M.A. NAYEEM, The United Arab Emirates [= Prehistory and Protohistory of the Arabian Peninsula, vol. III], Hyderabad, 1994, XXV + 332 p., var. fig., maps, Tab.

731 S. BLAU, Observing the present — reflecting the past. Attitudes towards archaeology in the United Arab Emirates, *in* Arabian archaeology and epigraphy 6/2, 1995, pp. 116-128, 2 fig.

732 P. HELLYER, Recorders' Reports. Archaeology, *in* Tribulus. Bulletin of the Emirates Natural History Group 5/1, 1995, p. 30.

733 P. HELLYER, Recorders' Reports. Archaeology, *in* Tribulus. Bulletin of the Emirates Natural History Group 5/2, 1995, p. 28.

Abu Dhabi

734 R. WESTERN, Qarn bint Saud, *in* Emirates Natural History Group (Abu Dhabi) Bulletin 18, November 1982, pp. 22-25, 3 fig.

735 L. COSTANTINI & L. COSTANTINI-BIASINI, Laboratory of Bioarchaeology, Palaeoethnobotanical Investigations in the Middle East and Arabian Peninsula, 1986: The United Arab Emirates, *in* East and West 36/4, 1986, pp. 355-360, fig. 5-8.

736 W.Y. al-TIKRITI, Archaeology in Al Ain, *in* Emirates Natural History Group (Abu Dhabi) Bulletin 30, November 1986, pp. 17-19, 1 map.

737 P. HELLYER, Relics of an Ancient Past, *in* The Land, its Heritage and People, *in* Abu Dhabi, Garden City of the Gulf (I. Fairservice & P. Hellyer, eds.), Dubai, 1988, pp. 26-28, 2 fig.

738 S. CLEUZIOU, Excavations at Hili 8: a preliminary report on the 4th to 7th campaigns, *in* Archaeology in the United Arab Emirates V, 1989, pp. 61-87, 2 Tab., Pl. 9-35.

739 B. VOGT, W. GOCKEL, H. HOFBAUER & A.A. al-HAY, The Coastal Survey in the Western Province of Abu Dhabi, 1983, *in* Archaeology in the United Arab Emirates V, 1989, pp. 49-60, Pl. 1-8.

740 P. HELLYER, New Discoveries at Dalma and Sir Bani Yas, *in* Arts & The Islamic World 23 [= Special issue: Architecture, Archaeology and the Arts in the United Arab Emirates], 1993, pp. 44-45.

741 P. HELLYER, New Discoveries on Dalma and Sir Bani Yas, *in* Tribulus. Bulletin of the Emirates Natural History Group 3/2, 1993, p. 16.

742 ANONYMUS, The copperindustry of Al Ain [= ADNOC and ADCO publication], al-Ain, 1994, 20 p., ill.

743 G.R.D. KING, D. DUNLOP, J. ELDERS, S. GARFI, A. STEPHENSON & C. TONGHINI, A report on the Abu Dhabi islands archaeological survey (1993-4), *in* Proceedings of the Seminar for Arabian Studies 25, [= Papers from the twenty-eighth meeting of the Seminar for Arabian Studies held in Oxford, 21–23 July 1994], 1995, pp. 63-74, 4 fig.

Sharjah

744 R. BOUCHARLAT, R. DALONGEVILLE, A. HESSE & P. SANLAVILLE, Survey in Sharjah Emirate, U.A.E. on behalf of the Department of Culture, Sharjah, First Report (1984), (N.H. al-Abboudi, ed.), Sharjah, 1989, 21 p., 12 fig., 17 Pl.

745 R. BOUCHARLAT & A. HESSE, Appendix 2: The Pottery, *in* 2nd Archaeological Survey in the Sharjah Emirate, 1985 — A Preliminary Report

(N.H. al-Abboudi & R. Boucharlat, eds.), Sharjah & Lyon, 1989, pp. 43-46, fig. 17-20, Pl. XI-XIII.

746 R. BOUCHARLAT et alii, Introduction, *in* 2nd Archaeological Survey in the Sharjah Emirate, 1985 — A Preliminary Report (N.H. al-Abboudi & R. Boucharlat, eds.), Sharjah & Lyon, 1989, pp. 7-8, fig. 1.

747 R. BOUCHARLAT et alii, Observations, *in* II. The Sharjah Coast, *in* 2nd Archaeological Survey in the Sharjah Emirate, 1985 — A Preliminary Report (N.H. al-Abboudi & R. Boucharlat, eds.), Sharjah & Lyon, 1989, pp. 26-33, fig. 5, 7, 11, 13, 20 & 21, Pl. Ia, II & IV.

748 R. BOUCHARLAT et alii, Conclusions, *in* 2nd Archaeological Survey in the Sharjah Emirate, 1985 — A Preliminary Report (N.H. al-Abboudi & R. Boucharlat, eds.), Sharjah & Lyon, 1989, pp. 38-42.

749 R. DALONGEVILLE & P. SANLAVILLE, Geographical Outline and Paleoenvironment, *in* 2nd Archaeological Survey in the Sharjah Emirate, 1985 — A Preliminary Report (N.H. al-Abboudi & R. Boucharlat, eds.), Sharjah & Lyon, 1989, pp. 9-15, fig. 2-15, Pl. I-IV.

750 A. HESSE, Methodology, *in* II. The Sharjah Coast, *in* 2nd Archaeological Survey in the Sharjah Emirate, 1985 — A Preliminary Report (N.H. al-Abboudi & R. Boucharlat, eds.), Sharjah & Lyon, 1989, pp. 16-17, fig. 11.

751 R. BOUCHARLAT, Introduction, *in* Archaeological Surveys and Excavations in the Sharjah Emirate, 1986. A Third Preliminary Report (N.H. al-Abboudi, ed.), Department of Culture & Information, Sharjah, 1990, pp. 7-10.

752 A. HESSE, The Sharjah Coast Survey, *in* Archaeological Surveys and Excavations in the Sharjah Emirate, 1986. A Third Preliminary Report (N.H. al-Abboudi, ed.), Department of Culture & Information, Sharjah, 1990, pp. 11-12, fig. 3, Tab. 1.

753 A. PRIEUR, Preliminary Remarks about Molluscs Fauna collected on the North Coast of the Sharjah Emirate in 1985, *in* Archaeological Surveys and Excavations in the Sharjah Emirate, 1986. A Third Preliminary Report (N.H. al-Abboudi, ed.), Department of Culture & Information, Sharjah, 1990, pp. 13-14.

754 R. BOUCHARLAT, Archaeological Research in the Emirate of Sharjah, *in* Tribulus. Bulletin of the Emirates Natural History Group 2/2, 1992, pp. 5-8.

755 R. BOUCHARLAT, Introduction, *in* Archaeological Surveys and Excavations in the Sharjah Emirate, 1990 and 1992. A Sixth Interim Report (R. Boucharlat, ed.), Lyon, 1992, pp. 1-2.

756 B. BRIAND, R. DALONGEVILLE & A. PLOQUIN, The industries of Mleiha mineralogical and archaeological data recovered from the site and its

environment in 1990, *in* Archaeological Surveys and Excavations in the Sharjah Emirate, 1990 and 1992. A Sixth Interim Report (R. Boucharlat, ed.), Lyon, 1992, pp. 45-48.

757 M. DRIEUX, Conservation in Sharjah: a brief assessment, *in* Archaeological Surveys and Excavations in the Sharjah Emirate, 1990 and 1992. A Sixth Interim Report (R. Boucharlat, ed.), Lyon, 1992, pp. 58-60.

758 M. MOUTON, Archaeological survey of the region of Al-Madam: preliminary results 1992, *in* Archaeological Surveys and Excavations in the Sharjah Emirate, 1990 and 1992. A Sixth Interim Report (R. Boucharlat, ed.), Lyon, 1992, pp. 3-10, fig. 1-4.

759 P. HUDSON, New Archaeological Museum at Sharjah, *in* Arts & The Islamic World 23 [= Special issue: Architecture, Archaeology and the Arts in the United Arab Emirates], 1993, pp. 56-57, 6 fig.

Umm al-Qaiwain

760 D.T. POTTS, Excavations at Tell Abraq, 1989, *in* Paléorient 15/1, 1989, pp. 269-271, 1 fig.

761 R. DALONGEVILLE, L'environnement du site de Tell Abraq, *in* D.T. Potts, Excavations at Tell Abraq, 1989: A Prehistoric Mound in the Emirate of Umm al-Qaiwain, U.A.E., Munksgaard–Copenhagen, 1990, pp. 125-126.

762 D.T. POTTS, A Prehistoric Mound in the Emirate of Umm al-Qaiwain, U.A.E. Excavations at Tell Abraq in 1989, Munksgaard–Copenhagen, 1990, 157 p., 156 fig.

763 A. PRIEUR, Etude faunistique et aspects anthropiques du site de Tell Abraq, *in* D.T. Potts, Excavations at Tell Abraq, 1989: A Prehistoric Mound in the Emirate of Umm al-Qaiwain, U.A.E., Munksgaard–Copenhagen, 1990, pp. 127-134.

764 C.H. PEDERSEN & V.F. BUCHWALD, An examination of metal objects from Tell Abraq, U.A.E., *in* Arabian archaeology and epigraphy 2/1, 1991, pp. 1-9, 7 fig., 2 Tab.

765 D.T. POTTS, Further Excavations at Tell Abraq. The 1990 Season, Munksgaard–Copenhagen, 1991, 155 p., 217 fig.

766 P. HELLYER, New Finds at Tell Abraq, *in* Tribulus. Bulletin of the Emirates Natural History Group 2/1, 1992, pp. 15-17, 2 fig.

767 E.C.L. DURING CASPERS, Review of D.T. Potts "A Prehistoric Mound in the Emirate of Umm al-Qaiwain, U.A.E. Excavations at Tell Abraq in 1989 with Contributions by Rémi Dalongeville and Abel Prieur", *in* Bibliotheca Orientalis L/5-6, 1993, pp. 728-735.

768 D.T. Potts, Excavations at Tell Abraq, *in* Arts & The Islamic World 23 [= Special issue: Architecture, Archaeology and the Arts in the United Arab Emirates], 1993, pp. 49-52, 9 fig.

769 D.T. Potts, Four seasons of excavations at Tell Abraq, *in* Proceedings of the Seminar for Arabian Studies 23 [= Proceedings of the 26th Seminar for Arabian Studies, held at Manchester 1992], 1993, pp. 117-126, 1 fig.

770 D.T. Potts, South and Central Asian elements at Tell Abraq (Emirate of Umm al-Qaiwain, United Arab Emirates), c. 2200 BC–AD 400, *in* South Asian Archaeology 1993. Proceedings of the Twelfth International Conference of the European Association of South Asian Archaeologists held in Helsinki University 5–9 July 1993 (A. Parpola & P. Koskikallio, eds.) [= Annales Academiae Scientiarum Fennicae, ser. B., Tom. 271], Vol. 2, Helsinki, 1994, pp. 615-628, 13 fig.

771 G. Willcox & M. Tengberg, Preliminary report on the archaeobotanical investigations at Tell Abraq with special attention to chaff impressions in mud brick, *in* Arabian archaeology and epigraphy 6/3, 1995, pp. 129-138, 4 fig., 1 Tab.

Ras al-Khaimah

772 M.J. Becker, Soft-Stone Analysis. Neutron Activation Analysis and Possible Identification of Sources for Objects Recovered During Archaeological Investigation. Technical Appendix 2 to P. Donaldson: Prehistoric Tombs of Ras al-Khaimah, *in* Oriens Antiquus XXIV/1-2, 1985, pp. 102-121, Tab. 11-15.

773 J.R. Cann, Examination of Thin Sections of Pottery from Site 1, Technical Appendix 4 to P. Donaldson: Prehistoric Tombs of Ras al-Khaimah, *in* Oriens Antiquus XXIV/1-2, 1985, pp. 125-126, Tab. 17.

774 J.R. Cann & C.K. Winter, X-Ray Fluorescence Analysis of Pottery from Site 1, Technical Appendix 3 to P. Donaldson: Prehistoric Tombs of Ras al-Khaimah, *in* Oriens Antiquus XXIV/1-2, 1985, pp. 122-124, Tab. 16.

775 P.T. Craddock, The Composition of the Metal Artifacts, Technical Appendix 1 to P. Donaldson: Prehistoric Tombs of Ras al-Khaimah, *in* Oriens Antiquus XXIV/1-2, 1985, pp. 97-101, Tab. 8-10.

776 B. De Cardi, Further Archaeological Survey in Ras al-Khaimah, U.A.E., 1977, *in* Oriens Antiquus XXIV/3, 1985, pp. 163-240, 17 fig., Pl. VIII-XV, 2 Tab.

777 P. Donaldson, Prehistoric Tombs of Ras al-Khaimah, *in* Oriens Antiquus XXIV/1-2, 1985, pp. 85-142, 5 fig., Tab VI-VII, 18 Tab.

778 K.R. SMYTHE, Mollusca, Technical Appendix 5 to P. Donaldson: Prehistoric Tombs of Ras al-Khaimah, *in* Oriens Antiquus XXIV/1-2, 1985, p. 127.

779 B. HERRMANN, Ras al-Khaimah, Emirats Arabes Unis: Shimal (I-III, 1985), *in* Lettre d'Information. Archéologie Orientale 8, 1986, p. 26.

780 B. VOGT, J. HÄSER & C. VELDE, Archäologische Forschungen in Shimal, Ras al-Khaimah (Vereinigte Arabische Emirate), *in* Archiv für Orientforschung XXXIV, 1987, pp. 237-242, 4 Abb.

781 B. VOGT, U. FRANKE-VOGT, J.-M. KÄSTNER, C. VELDE, S. MERY, H. SCHUTKOWSKI, B. HERRMANN & J. HÄSER, Shimal 1985/1986. Excavations of the German Archaeological Mission in Ras al-Khaimah, U.A.E. — A Preliminary Report [= Berliner Beiträge zum Vorderen Orient 8], Berlin, 1987, 126 p., 51 fig., 32 Pl.

782 ANONYMUS, National Museum of Ras al Khaimah, Ras al Khaimah, U.A.E., 1988, 68 p., 28 fig., 2 plans.

783 B. VOGT, J. HÄSER, J.-M. KÄSTNER, H. SCHUTKOWSKI & C. VELDE, Preliminary Remarks on two recently excavated Tombs in Shimal, Ras al-Khaimah, *in* South Asian Archaeology 1985 (K. Frifelt & P. Sørensen, eds.) [= Scandinavian Institute of Asian Studies Occasional Papers 4 — Papers from the Eighth International Conference of South Asian Archaeologists in Western Europe, Moesgaard, 1985], London & Riverdale, 1989, pp. 62-73, 10 fig.

784 J. HÄSER, Soft-Stone Vessels from Shimal and Dhayah (Ras al-Khaimah, U.A.E.), *in* Gedenkschrift für Jürgen Driehaus (F.M. Andraschko & W.-R. Teegen, eds.), Mainz, 1990, pp. 347-355, 3 fig.

785 J.-M. KÄSTNER, Die 4. Kampagne der Deutschen Archäologischen Mission Ras al-Khaimah, *in* The Arabian Gulf Gazetteer I,1 (E.C.L. During Caspers, ed.), Leiden, 1990, p. 17, 1 fig.

786 S. KAY, A Long History, *in* Portrait of Ras al Khaimah, Dubai, 1990, pp. 50-69, var. fig.

787 H. SCHUTKOWSKI, Possibilities of Anthropological Interpretation in Disturbed Collective Burials, *in* South Asian Archaeology 1987 [= Proceedings of the Ninth International Conference of the Association of South Asian Archaeologists in Western Europe held in the Fondazione Giorgio Cini, Venice (M. Taddei, ed.)], Rome, 1990, pp. 555-568, 11 fig.

788 H. DAVID, A first petrographic description of the soft stone vessels from Shimal, *in* Golf–Archäologie. Mesopotamien, Iran, Kuwait, Bahrain, Vereinigte Arabische Emirate und Oman (K. Schippmann, A. Herling & J.-F. Salles, eds.) [= Internationale Archäologie 6, Buch am Erlbach], Göttingen & Lyon, 1991, pp. 175-178, 1 Tab.

789 U. FRANKE-VOGT, The settlement of Central-Shimal, *in* Golf–Archäologie. Mesopotamien, Iran, Kuwait, Bahrain, Vereinigte Arabische Emirate und Oman (K. Schippmann, A. Herling & J.-F. Salles, eds.) [= Internationale Archäologie 6, Buch am Erlbach], Göttingen & Lyon, 1991, pp. 179-204, 9 fig., 2 Pl., 1 Tab.

790 E. GLOVER, The molluscan fauna from Shimal, Ras al-Khaimah, United Arab Emirates, *in* Golf–Archäologie. Mesopotamien, Iran, Kuwait, Bahrain, Vereinigte Arabische Emirate und Oman (K. Schippmann, A. Herling & J.-F. Salles, eds.) [= Internationale Archäologie 6, Buch am Erlbach], Göttingen & Lyon, 1991, pp. 205-220, 2 fig., 1 Pl., 3 Tab.

791 J. HÄSER, Soft-stone vessels from Shimal and Dhayah / Ras al-Khaimah, U.A.E., *in* Golf–Archäologie. Mesopotamien, Iran, Kuwait, Bahrain, Vereinigte Arabische Emirate und Oman (K. Schippmann, A. Herling & J.-F. Salles, eds.) [= Internationale Archäologie 6, Buch am Erlbach], Göttingen & Lyon, 1991, pp. 221-232, 3 fig.

792 B. DE CARDI, D. KENNET & R.L. STOCKS, Five thousand years of settlement at Khatt, UAE, *in* Proceedings of the Seminar for Arabian Studies 24 [= Proceedings of the 27th Seminar for Arabian Studies held in London on 22–24 July 1993], 1994, pp. 35-96, 15 fig., XV Pl., Tab.

793 J. KUNKEL, Appendix: Die Metallfunde aus Asimah, Ras al-Khaimah, *in* B. Vogt, Asimah. An Account of a Two Months Rescue Excavation in the Mountains of Ras al-Khaimah, United Arab Emirates (Dept. of Antiquities and Museums, Ras al-Khaimah), Dubai, 1994, pp. 187-204.

794 B. VOGT, Asimah. An Account of a Two Months Rescue Excavation in the Mountains of Ras al-Khaimah, United Arab Emirates (Dept. of Antiquities and Museums, Ras al-Khaimah), Dubai, 1994, vii+214 p., 81 fig., 25 Pl.

Fujairah

795 P. CORBOUD, R. HAPKA & P. IM-OBERSTEG, Archaeological Survey of Fujairah, 1 (1987). Preliminary Report First Campaign of the Archaeological Survey of Fujairah (United Arab Emirates) — Rapport préliminaire de la première campagne de survey archéologique du Fujairah (Emirats Arabes Unis), Berne, Vaduz, Genève & Neuchâtel, 1988, 72 p., 12 fig.

796 P. CORBOUD, Archaeological Survey of Fujairah. Swiss-Liechtenstein Foundation for Archaeological Research Abroad. Compte-Rendu de la campagne 1989 du Survey archéologique du Fujairah (U.A.E.), *in* The Arabian Gulf Gazetteer I,1 (E.C.L. During Caspers, ed.), Leiden, 1990, pp. 18-19, 6 fig.

797 P. CORBOUD, A.-C. CASTELLA, R. HAPKA & P. IM-OBERSTEG, Archaeological Survey of Fujairah, 2 (1988-1989), Preliminary Report Second and Third Campaigns of the Archaeological Survey of Fujairah (United Arab Emirates) — Rapport préliminaire des deuxième et troisième campagnes du Survey archéologique du Fujairah (E.A.U.), Berne, Vaduz, Genève & Neuchâtel, 1990, 118 p., 30 fig.

798 P. HELLYER, A Distant Past, *in* Fujairah. An Arabian Jewel, Dubai, 1990, pp. 40-49, 10 fig.

799 P. CORBOUD, Survey archéologique du Fujairah (E.A.U.). Compte rendu des troisième et quatrième campagnes de recherches: novembre-décembre 1989 et décembre-janvier 1990-91, Genève, 1991, 32 p., 14 fig.

800 P. CORBOUD, A.C. CASTELLA, R. HAPKA & P. IM-OBERSTEG, Rapport préliminaire de la campagne 1993 du survey archéologique de Fujairah (E.A.U.), Berne, 1994, 39 p., var. fig.

801 M. JONGBLOED, Petroglyphs in Wadi Ashwani, Fujairah, *in* Tribulus. Bulletin of the Emirates Natural History Group 4/2, 1994, p. 24, 2 fig. (p. 19).

802 L. BRASS, R. PAINTER, G. BRITTON & L. HILL, Fujairah Archaeological Survey. An Interim Report, *in* Tribulus. Bulletin of the Emirates Natural History Group 5/1, 1995, pp. 11-13.

Oman

803 G. WEISGERBER, Beispiele zu Problemen und Möglichkeiten bergbauarchäologischer Forschungen, *in* Mineralische Rohstoffe als kulturhistorische Informationsquelle (H.W. Hennicker, ed.), Hagen, 1978, pp. 19-35.

804 G. WEISGERBER, A new kind of Copper Slag from Tawi Aarja, Oman, *in* Journal of Historical Metallurgy Society 1, 1978, pp. 40-43, 6 fig.

805 G. WEISGERBER, Patterns of Early Islamic Metallurgy in Oman, *in* Proceedings of the Seminar for Arabian Studies 10 [= Proceedings of the 13th Seminar for Arabian Studies 1979], 1980, pp. 115-126, 11 fig.

806 T. BERTHOUD & S. CLEUZIOU, Archéologie et archéométrie: les leçons d'une expérience, *in* De l'Indus aux Balkans, Recueil à la Mémoire de Jean Deshayes (J.-L. Huot, M. Yon & Y. Calvet, eds.), Paris, 1985, pp. 29-42.

807 A. HAUPTMANN, 5000 Jahre Kupfer in Oman. Band 1. Die Entwicklung der Kupfermetallurgie vom 3. Jahrtausend bis zur Neuzeit, *in* Der Anschnitt, Beiheft 4, Bochum, 1985, 137 p., 83 Abb.

808 J.J. ORCHARD & J.C. ORCHARD, The University of Birmingham Archaeological Expedition to the Sultanate of Oman: Three seasons of work in the Wadi Bahla, 1980-1984, Birmingham, 1985, 25 p., 8 fig., 24 Pl.

809 P. Yule & G. Weisgerber, The First Metal Hoard in Oman, *in* American Journal of Archaeology 90, 1986, p. 223.

810 P.M. Costa & T.J. Wilkinson, The Development of Settlement and the Regional Economy, *in* The Hinterland of Sohar. Archaeological Surveys and Excavations within the Region of an Omani Seafaring City (P.M. Costa & T.J. Wilkinson, eds.), *in* The Journal of Oman Studies 9, 1987, pp. 223-234, fig. 110.

811 P.M. Costa. & T.J. Wilkinson, The Finds (Zahra & 'Arja), *in* The Hinterland of Sohar. Archaeological Surveys and Excavations within the Region of an Omani Seafaring City (P.M. Costa & T.J. Wilkinson, eds.), *in* The Journal of Oman Studies 9, 1987, pp. 173-210, fig. 86-106, Pl. 110-113.

812 P.M. Costa & T.J. Wilkinson, Settlement and Copper Exploitation in the 'Arja Area, *in* The Hinterland of Sohar. Archaeological Surveys and Excavations within the Region of an Omani Seafaring City (P.M. Costa & T.J. Wilkinson, eds.), *in* The Journal of Oman Studies 9, 1987, pp. 93-131, fig. 33-57.

813 G. Santini, Site RH-10 at Qurum and a Preliminary Analysis of Its Cemetery: An Essay in Stratigraphic Discontinuity, *in* Proceedings of the Seminar for Arabian Studies 17 [= Proceedings of the 20th Seminar for Arabian Studies 1986], 1987, pp. 179-198, 12 fig.

814 G. Weisgerber, Archaeological Evidence of Copper Exploitation at 'Arja, *in* The Hinterland of Sohar. Archaeological Surveys and Excavations within the Region of an Omani Seafaring City (P.M. Costa & T.J. Wilkinson, eds.), *in* The Journal of Oman Studies 9, 1987, pp. 145-172, fig. 64-85, Pl. 74-109.

815 Anonymus, The Oman Museum, Sultanate of Oman. Handbook for Visitors. Le Musée d'Oman, Sultanat d'Oman. Un livret du Musée, Muscat, 1988, 36 p., fig.

816 A. Hauptmann, G. Weisgerber & H.G. Bachmann, Early Copper Metallurgy in Oman, *in* The Beginning of the Use of Metals and Alloys (R. Maddin, ed.), Cambridge, Mass., 1988, pp. 34-51, fig. 4:1-13, Tab. 4:1-4.

817 S. Kay, Enchanting Oman, Dubai, 1988, 123 p., var. fig.

818 L. Bondioli, The Use of Advanced Technologies in the Hadd Program: Computer as a Tool for the Archaeologist, *in* The Joint Hadd Project. Summary Report on the Second Season. November 1986–January 1987 (S. Cleuziou & M. Tosi, eds.), 1989, pp. 81-82.

819 S. Cleuziou & M. Tosi, A Short Report on the Excavations of the Second Campaign at RJ-2, *in* The Joint Hadd Project. Summary Report on the Second Season. November 1986–January 1987 (S. Cleuziou & M. Tosi, eds.), 1989, pp. 11-26, fig. 7-23.

820 M. COLTORTI, Geomorphological characteristics of the Ras al-Junayz area (Sultanate of Oman), *in* Oman Studies, Papers on the archaeology and history of Oman [= Serie Orientale Roma 63 (P.M. Costa & M. Tosi, eds.)], Roma, 1989, pp. 79-96, 8 fig.

821 P.M. COSTA, Historical interpretation of the territory of Muscat, *in* Oman Studies, Papers on the archaeology and history of Oman [= Serie Orientale Roma 63 (P.M. Costa & M. Tosi, eds.)], Roma, 1989, pp. 97-117, 1fig., 18 Pl.

822 C. EDENS, Preliminary Archaeological Survey at the Ja'alan Interior, *in* The Joint Hadd Project. Summary Report on the Second Season. November 1986–January 1987 (S. Cleuziou & M. Tosi, eds.), 1989, pp. 64-74, fig. 54-59.

823 M. MASSOUBRE, A Short Report on the Geology of the Ra's al-Hadd Area, *in* The Joint Hadd Project. Summary Report on the Second Season. November 1986–January 1987 (S. Cleuziou & M. Tosi, eds.), 1989, pp. 78-80, fig. 63-64.

824 S. PRACCHIA, Elements of a Detailed Stratigraphical Analysis at RJ-2, *in* The Joint Hadd Project. Summary Report on the Second Season. November 1986–January 1987 (S. Cleuziou & M. Tosi, eds.), 1989, pp. 30-32, fig. 27.

825 M. TOSI, Protohistoric archaeology in Oman: the first thirty years (1956-1985), *in* Oman Studies, Papers on the archaeology and history of Oman [= Serie Orientale Roma 63 (P.M. Costa & M. Tosi, eds.)], Roma, 1989, pp. 135-161, 1 Pl.

826 G. WEISGERBER & P. YULE, The First Metal Hoard in Oman, *in* South Asian Archaeology 1985 (K. Frifelt & P. Sørensen, eds.) [= Scandinavian Institute of Asian Studies Occasional Papers 4 — Papers from the Eighth International Conference of South Asian Archaeologists in Western Europe, Moesgaard, 1985], London & Riverdale, 1989, pp. 60-61, 1 fig.

827 P. YULE & G. WEISGERBER, Tales from Mazoon, *in* PDO News [= Petroleum Development Oman News], Muscat, 1989-2, pp. 9-13, 14 fig.

828 S. CLEUZIOU & M. TOSI, The third campaign at RJ-2. A Preliminary Report, *in* The Joint Hadd Project. Summary Report on the Third Season. October 1987–February 1988 (S. Cleuziou, J. Reade & M. Tosi, eds.), 1990, pp. 11-27, fig. 7-24.

829 H. DAVID, M. TEGYEY, J. LE METOUR & R. WYNS, Les vases en chlorites dans la péninsule d'Oman: une étude pétrographique appliquée à l'archéologie, *in* Comptes-Rendus de l'Académie des Sciences 311, série II, Paris, 1990, pp. 951-958, 4 fig.

830 C. EDENS, Brief Survey Around Bilad Bani Bu Hassan, *in* The Joint Hadd Project. Summary Report on the Third Season. October 1987–February 1988 (S. Cleuziou, J. Reade & M. Tosi, eds.), 1990, pp. 44-55, fig. 40-45.

831 W. LANCASTER & F. LANCASTER, Anthropological survey at Ra's al-Junayz: a first preliminary report, *in* The Joint Hadd Project. Summary

Report on the Third Season. October 1987–February 1988 (S. Cleuziou, J. Reade & M. Tosi, eds.), 1990, pp. 56-65.

832 R. NISBET, Macrobotanical aspects of RJ-1 and RJ-2 (excavations 1986-88), *in* The Joint Hadd Project. Summary Report on the Third Season. October 1987–February 1988 (S. Cleuziou, J. Reade & M. Tosi, eds.), 1990, pp. 31-32.

833 J. READE, Excavations at Ra's al-Hadd, 1988: Preliminary Report, *in* The Joint Hadd Project. Summary Report on the Third Season. October 1987–February 1988 (S. Cleuziou, J. Reade & M. Tosi, eds.), 1990, pp. 33-43, fig. 29-39.

834 S. KAY, A turbulent past, *in* Sultanate of Oman, *in* Arabian Profiles. The Arab Gulf Cooperation Council (AGCC) — Bahrain, Kuwait, Oman, Qatar, Saudi Arabia & UAE (I. Fairservice & C. Grieve, eds.), Dubai, 1991, pp. 65-67.

835 G. WEISGERBER, Archäologisches Fundgut des 2. Jahrtausends v. Chr. in Oman. Möglichkeiten zur Chronologischen Gliederung?, *in* Golf–Archäologie. Mesopotamien, Iran, Kuwait, Bahrain, Vereinigte Arabische Emirate und Oman (K. Schippmann, A. Herling & J.-F. Salles, eds.) [= Internationale Archäologie 6, Buch am Erlbach], Göttingen & Lyon, 1991, pp. 321-330, 4 Abb.

836 S. BÖKÖNYI, Preliminary Information on the Faunal Remains from Excavations at Ras al-Junayz (Oman), *in* South Asian Archaeology 1989 [= Papers from the Tenth International Conference of South Asian Archaeologists in Western Europe, Musée national des Arts asiatiques–Guimet, Paris, France, 3-7 July 1989 (C. Jarrige, ed. with the assistance of J.P. Gerry & R.H. Meadow)], [= Monographs in World Archaeology n°. 14], Madison, 1992, pp. 45-48, 3 fig.

837 ANONYMUS, Oman's Archaeological Treasures, *in* PDO News [= Petroleum Development News], Muscat, 1994-1, pp. 22-28, var. ill.

838 S. MERY, Intégration de la céramique dans la culture matérielle de l'Arabie Orientale et réseaux d'échanges protohistoriques: la céramique mésopotamienne en Oman de la fin du 6e au milieu du 2e millénaire, *in* Orient Express. Notes et Nouvelles d'Archéologie Orientale 3, décembre 1994, pp. 96-99, 1 fig., 1 Tab.

839 I. GUBA, Tablets of Stone, *in* PDO News [= Petroleum Development Oman News], Muscat, 1995-2, pp. 14-19, var. ill.

840 P. YULE & C. RÖSCH, Pre-islamic beads from the Sultanate of Oman: A mineralogical Study, *in* Bead Study Trust Newsletter 26, 1995, p. 12.

841 A.H. al-MALALLAH, Outline of the History of Oman, Muscat, s.d., 25 p., 19 fig., 1 map.

PREHISTORY — 4TH MILLENNIUM B.C.

General studies

842 B. DE CARDI, Some aspects of Neolithic settlement in Bahrain and adjacent regions, *in* Bahrain through the ages, the Archaeology (Shaikha Haya Ali al-Khalifa & M. Rice, eds.), London, 1986, pp. 87-93.

843 J. OATES, The Gulf in Prehistory, *in* Bahrain through the ages, the Archaeology (Shaikha Haya Ali al-Khalifa & M. Rice, eds.), London, 1986, pp. 79-86, fig. 21-22.

844 J. TIXIER, The prehistory of the Gulf: recent finds, *in* Bahrain through the ages, the Archaeology (Shaikha Haya Ali al-Khalifa & M. Rice, eds.), London, 1986, pp. 76-78.

845 H.G. GEBEL, Südostarabien. Prähistorische Besiedlung, *in* Tübinger Atlas des Vorderen Orients, Karten BI 8.3.1 (Steinzeit der Omanischen Halbinsel), Wiesbaden, 1988.

846 K. FRIFELT, 'Ubaid in the Gulf Area, *in* Upon this Foundation — The 'Ubaid Reconsidered (E.F. Henrickson & I. Thuesen, eds.) [= Carsten Niebuhr Institute Publications 10], Copenhagen, 1989, pp. 404-417, 6 fig.

847 P.R.S. MOOREY, From Gulf to Delta in the Fourth Millennium B.C.: The Syrian Connection, *in* Eretz-Israel 21 [= Amiran Festschrift], 1990, pp. 62-69.

848 F. HOLE, Environmental Instabilities and Urban Origins, *in* Chiefdoms and Early States in the Near East. The Organizational Dynamics of Complexity (G. Stein & M.S. Rothman, eds.) [= Monographs in World Archaeology n°. 18], Madison, 1994, pp. 121-151, 10 fig.

849 M. ROAF & J. GALBRAITH, Pottery and p-values: 'Seafaring merchants of Ur?', re-examined, *in* Antiquity 68, 1994, pp. 770-783, 4 fig., 2 Tab.

Kuwait

850 H. FIELD, Kuwait, *in* Reconnaissance in Southwestern Asia, *in* Southwestern Journal of Anthropology 7, 1951, pp. 92-93.

851 F. HOURS, Assemblage provenant de Burgan Basin, Kuwait, *in* Y. Calvet & J.-F. Salles, Bibliographical notes, *in* Failaka. Fouilles françaises 1986-1988 (Y. Calvet & J. Gachet, eds.) [= Travaux de la Maison de l'Orient 18], Lyon, 1990, p. 13.

Northeastern Arabia

852 B.D. Hermansen, 'Ubaid and ED pottery from five sites at 'Ain as-Sayh, Saudi Arabia, *in* Arabian archaeology and epigraphy 4/2, 1993, pp. 126-144, 29 fig., 3 Tab.

853 H.A. McClure & N.Y. al-Shaikh, Palaeogeography of an 'Ubaid archaeological site, Saudi Arabia, *in* Arabian archaeology and epigraphy 4/2, 1993, pp. 107-125, 20 fig.

Qatar

854 J. Desse, Etude de l'ichthyofaune et des macromammifères du site de Khor F.B. (Qatar, Golfe Arabique): méthodologie et résultats préliminaires, *in* Recherches anthropologiques Proche et Moyen Orient, 1980, pp. 44-80.

855 J. Desse, Analyse des vestiges osseux de Khor P. (Qatar). Résultats préliminaires, *in* Recherches anthropologiques Proche et Moyen-Orient, 1980, pp. 70-77.

856 C. Bahezre, Perle en obsidienne de Khor, *in* Paléorient 11/1, 1985, p. 140.

857 B. Midant-Reynes, Un ensemble de sépultures en fosses sous cairn à Khor (Qatar): Etude de rites funéraires, *in* Paléorient 11/1, 1985, pp. 129-139, 6 fig., 4 Tab., 2 Pl.

858 B. Piriou, Perle en obsidienne de Khor I, *in* Paléorient 11/1, 1985, p. 140.

859 A.-M. Tillier, Tumulus de Khor — Etude anthropologique, *in* Paléorient 11/1, 1985, pp. 141-144, II Tabl.

860 R. Bonnefille & G. Riollet, Palynologie des sédiments holocènes de sites archéologiques du Qatar — Palynology of archaeological sites from Qatar, *in* M.-L. Inizan, Préhistoire à Qatar. Mission archéologique française à Qatar, Tome 2, Paris, 1988, pp. 137-145 & 221, 4 fig.

861 L. Courtois & B. Velde, Rapport sur l'analyse à la microsonde électronique des peintures ornant quatre céramiques de type obeidien du Qatar (Khor) — Report concerning electron microprobe analyses of surface on Ubaid (3-4) ceramics from Qatar, *in* M.-L. Inizan, Préhistoire à Qatar. Mission archéologique française à Qatar, Tome 2, Paris, 1988, pp. 151-155 & 223-224, 2 fig.

862 J. Desse, Khor "P", Khor "F.B" et "Shagra". Les faunes. Le rôle de la pêche — Fish remains and macromammalian fauna from Khor and Shagra. Methodology and preliminary results, *in* M.-L. Inizan, Préhistoire à Qatar. Mission archéologique française à Qatar, Tome 2, Paris, 1988, pp. 157-165 & 225-226, 2 fig.

863 P. GEHIN, Hypothèses relatives à l'évolution géomorphologique et au bilan géopédologique du quaternaire récent de la péninsule de Qatar — Late Quaternary morphological evolution and geopedology in the Qatar peninsula: some hypotheses, *in* M.-L. Inizan, Préhistoire à Qatar. Mission archéologique française à Qatar, Tome 2, Paris, 1988, pp. 167-184 & 227-228, 12 fig.

864 J.-J. HUBLIN, A.-M. TILLIER & B. VANDERMEERSCH, Etude du squelette humain découvert à Khor (Qatar) — Discovery of a human skeleton at Khor (Qatar), *in* M.-L. Inizan, Préhistoire à Qatar. Mission archéologique française à Qatar, Tome 2, Paris, 1988, pp. 185-194 & 229, 8 fig.

865 M.-L. INIZAN, Préhistoire à Qatar — Prehistory in Qatar. Mission archéologique française à Qatar, Tome 2, Paris, 1988, pp. 16-136 & 197-220, 56 fig.

866 M. RICQ DE BOUARD, Analyses minéralogiques et pétrographiques d'échantillons archéologiques de Qatar — Mineralogical analyses of pottery, *in* M.-L. Inizan, Préhistoire à Qatar. Mission archéologique française à Qatar, Tome 2, Paris, 1988, pp. 195-196 & 230.

United Arab Emirates

867 E. HAERINCK, More prehistoric finds from the United Arab Emirates, *in* Arabian archaeology and epigraphy 5/3, 1994, pp. 153-157, 8 fig.

Abu Dhabi

868 R. WESTERN, A New Flint Find in Abu Dhabi, *in* Emirates Natural History Group (Abu Dhabi) Bulletin 10, March 1980, pp. 19-22, 3 fig.

869 H.G. GEBEL, Evidence for Pre-Holocene Industries in the Greater Hili Area, *in* Emirates Natural History Group (Abu Dhabi) Bulletin 23, July 1984, pp. 7-10, 2 fig.

870 R. WESTERN, Flint Finds from Jebel Mahijir, Abu Dhabi, *in* Emirates Natural History Group (Abu Dhabi) Bulletin 36, November 1988, pp. 27-28, 8 fig.

871 H.G. GEBEL, C. HANSS, A. LIEBAU & W. RAEHLE, The Late Quaternary Environments of 'Ain al-Faidha/Al-'Ain, Abu Dhabi Emirate, *in* Archaeology in the United Arab Emirates V, 1989, pp. 9-48, 5 Tab., 12 fig., 6 Pl.

872 P. STOEL, Al Hair Archaeological Site, *in* Emirates Natural History Group (Abu Dhabi) Bulletin 41, July 1990, pp. 25-28, var. fig.

873 ANONYMUS, Neolithic flints from Merawah, *in* Tribulus. Bulletin of the Emirates Natural History Group 3/1, 1993, p. 20, 1 fig.

874 S. MCBREARTY, Lithic artifacts from Abu Dhabi's Western Region, *in* Tribulus. Bulletin of the Emirates Natural History Group 3/1, 1993, pp. 13-14, 2 fig.

875 K. FLAVIN & E. SHEPHERD, Fishing in the Gulf: Preliminary investigations at an Ubaid site, Dalma (UAE), *in* Proceedings of the Seminar for Arabian Studies 24 [= Proceedings of the 27th Seminar for Arabian Studies held in London on 22–24 July 1993], 1994, pp. 115-134, 10 fig., 3 Tab.

Sharjah

876 M.-C. CAUVIN & S. CALLEY, Preliminary Report on Lithic Material, Appendix 1 to R. Boucharlat, R. Dalongeville, A. Hesse & P. Sanlaville, Survey in Sharjah Emirate, U.A.E. on behalf of the Department of Culture, Sharjah, First Report (1984), (N.H. al-Abboudi, ed.), Sharjah, 1989, pp. 17-19, fig. 9-12.

877 A. MINZONI DEROCHE, The Prehistoric Periods: The Artefacts, *in* II. The Sharjah Coast, *in* 2nd Archaeological Survey in the Sharjah Emirate, 1985 — A Preliminary Report (N.H. al-Abboudi & R. Boucharlat, eds.), Sharjah & Lyon, 1989, pp. 18-19.

878 A. MINZONI DEROCHE, The Inland Plain: Archaeological Surveys — Survey on Prehistoric Sites, *in* 2nd Archaeological Survey in the Sharjah Emirate, 1985 — A Preliminary Report (N. H. al-Abboudi & R. Boucharlat, eds.), Sharjah & Lyon, 1989, pp. 34-36, fig. 29-31, Pl. XIV-XV, Tabl. 1-2.

879 S. CALLEY & M.-A. SANTONI, Sounding at the Prehistoric Site al-Qassimiya, *in* Archaeological Surveys and Excavations in the Sharjah Emirate, 1986. A Third Preliminary Report (N.H. al-Abboudi, ed.), Department of Culture & Information, Sharjah, 1990, pp. 15-16, fig. 4, Pl. I a-b.

880 S. CALLEY & M.-A. SANTONI, A Prehistoric Site in Mleiha Area (P28): A Short Note, *in* Archaeological Surveys and Excavations in the Sharjah Emirate, 1986. A Third Preliminary Report (N.H. al-Abboudi, ed.), Department of Culture & Information, Sharjah, 1990, pp. 24-25, fig. 7.

881 S. CALLEY, R. DALONGEVILLE, P. SANLAVILLE & M.-A. SANTONI, The Dhaid-Fili Plain — Geomorphology and Prehistory, *in* Archaeological Surveys and Excavations in the Sharjah Emirate, 1986. A Third Preliminary Report (N.H. al-Abboudi, ed.), Department of Culture & Information, Sharjah, 1990, pp. 17-23, fig. 2-10, Pl. II-VI.

882 R. BOUCHARLAT, R. DALONGEVILLE, A. HESSE & M. MILLET, Occupation humaine et environnement au 5e et au 4e millénaire sur la côte Sharjah–Umm al Qaiwain (U.A.E.), *in* Arabian archaeology and epigraphy 2/2, 1991, pp. 93-106, 3 fig.

Ajman

883 E. HAERINCK, Heading for the Straits of Hormuz, an 'Ubaid site in the Emirate of Ajman (U.A.E.), *in* Arabian archaeology and epigraphy 2/2, 1991, pp. 84-90, 9 fig.

884 M. MILLET, Comments on the lithic material from an 'Ubaid site in the Emirate of Ajman (U.A.E.), *in* Arabian archaeology and epigraphy 2/2, 1991, pp. 91-92, 1 fig.

Umm al-Qaiwain

885 R. BOUCHARLAT, E. HAERINCK, C.S. PHILLIPS & D.T. POTTS, Note on an Ubaid-pottery site in the Emirate of Umm al-Qaiwain, *in* Arabian archaeology and epigraphy 2/2, 1991, pp. 65-71, 4 fig.

886 A. PRIEUR & C. GUERIN, Découverte d'un site préhistorique d'abattage de dugongs à Umm al-Qaiwain (Emirats Arabes Unis), *in* Arabian archaeology and epigraphy 2/2, 1991, pp. 72-83, 6 fig.

Ras al-Khaimah

887 B. VOGT, In search of coastal sites in pre-historic Makkan: Mid Holocene "shell-eaters" in the coastal desert of Ras al-Khaimah, U.A.E., *in* From Sumer to Meluhha: Contributions to the Archaeology of South and West Asia in Memory of George F. Dales (J. M. Kenoyer, ed.) [= Wisconsin Archaeological Reports 3], Madison, 1994, pp. 113-128, 5 fig.

Oman

888 P. BIAGI, R. NISBET & R. MAGGI, Oman: Excavations at the RH 5 Settlement, Qurum, Winter 1984-1985, *in* East and West 34, 1984, pp. 455-465, 8 fig.

889 P. Biagi, W. Torke, M. Tosi & H.-P. Uerpmann, Qurum: a case study of coastal archaeology in Northern Oman, *in* World Archaeology 16/1, 1984, pp. 43-61, 6 fig., 2 Tab., 1 Pl.

890 P. Biagi, Excavation of the Aceramic Shell Midden of RH 6, Qurum, Muscat, *in* East and West 35/4, 1985, pp. 410-415, fig. 3-7.

891 P. Biagi & R.A. Travers, Non-Mammalian Osteological Remains and Fishing Implements at RH 5 and RH 6, Muscat, *in* East and West 35/4, 1985, pp. 407-410.

892 A. Coppa, R. Macchiarelli, S. Salvatori & G. Santini, The Prehistoric Graveyard of Ra's al Hamra (RH 5): A short preliminary report on the 1981-83 excavations, *in* The Journal of Oman Studies 8/1, 1985, pp. 97-102, 2 fig., 4 Pl.

893 R. Maggi, RH 6-1985-1986 Campaign. The chipped Stone Industry, *in* East and West 35/4, 1985, pp. 407-408, 2 fig.

894 R. Nisbet, Evidence of Sorghum at site RH 5, Qurum (Muscat, Oman), *in* East and West 35/4, 1985, pp. 415-417, fig. 8-9.

895 J. Pullar, A Selection of Aceramic Sites in the Sultanate of Oman, *in* The Journal of Oman Studies 7, 1985, pp. 49-87, 16 fig., 7 charts, 11 Pl.

896 P. Biagi & S. Salvatori, Gli Scavi nell' Insediamento preistorico e nella necropoli di Ra's al Hamra 5 (Muscat — Oman), 1980-1985, *in* Rivista di Archeologia X, 1986, pp. 5-14, 14 fig.

897 F. Ghisotti, Shell Finds in the Course of the Archaeological Excavations at Ra's al-Hamra, *in* East and West 36/4, 1986, pp. 471-472, 1 fig.

898 P. Biagi, The Prehistoric Fishermen Settlements of RH 5 and RH 6 at Qurum, Sultanate of Oman, *in* Proceedings of the Seminar for Arabian Studies 17 [= Proceedings of the 20th Seminar for Arabian Studies 1986], 1987, pp. 15-19, 3 fig.

899 P. Biagi, Surveys along the Oman coast: preliminary report on the 1985-1988 campaigns, *in* East and West 38/1-4, 1988, pp. 271-291, 17 fig.

900 C. Edens, Archaeology of the Sands and Adjacent Portions of the Sharqiyah, *in* The Scientific Results of the Royal Geographical Society's Oman Wahiba Sands Project, 1985-1987 (R.W. Dutton, ed.), [= The Journal of Oman Studies Special Report 3], London, 1988, pp. 113-130, 12 fig., 4 Tab.

901 P. Biagi, The Excavations of Structure 5 at RJ-1, *in* The Joint Hadd Project. Summary Report on the Second Season. November 1986–January 1987 (S. Cleuziou & M. Tosi, eds.), 1989, pp. 5-10, fig. 1-6.

902 P. Biagi, D.A. Jones & R. Nisbet, A Preliminary Report on the Excavation of Structure 5 at Ra's al-Junayz 1 (Sultanate of Oman), *in* Rivista di Archeologia XIII, 1989, pp. 18-30, 7 fig., 1 Pl.

903 P. Biagi & R. Maggi, Prehistoric Surveys carried out in the Winter of 1986/1987 along the Oman Coast, *in* The Joint Hadd Project. Summary Report on the Second Season. November 1986–January 1987 (S. Cleuziou & M. Tosi, eds.), 1989, pp. 56-63, fig. 46-53.

904 P. Biagi, R. Maggi & R. Nisbet, Excavations at the aceramic coastal settlement of RH 5 (Muscat, Sultanate of Oman) 1983-85, *in* South Asian Archaeology 1985 (K. Frifelt & P. Sørensen, eds.) [= Scandinavian Institute of Asian Studies Occasional Papers 4 — Papers from the Eighth International Conference of South Asian Archaeologists in Western Europe, Moesgaard, 1985], London & Riverdale, 1989, pp. 1-8, 6 fig., 1 Tab.

905 P. Biagi & R. Nisbet, Some aspects of the 1982-1985 excavations at the aceramic coastal settlement of RH 5 at Qurm (Muscat-Sultanate of Oman), *in* Oman Studies, Papers on the archaeology and history of Oman [= Serie Orientale Roma 63 (P.M. Costa & M. Tosi, eds.)], Roma, 1989, pp. 31-46, 8 fig.

906 V. Charpentier, Short Preliminary Report on Lithic Artifacts at Ra's al-Junayz, *in* The Joint Hadd Project. Summary Report on the Second Season. November 1986–January 1987 (S. Cleuziou & M. Tosi, eds.), 1989, pp. 48-50, fig. 39-40.

907 E. Isetti & P. Biagi, The Polished Stone Earrings of Site RH 5 and the Distribution and Chronology of Prehistoric Earrings of Coastal Oman, *in* Rivista di Archeologia XIII, 1989, pp. 5-17, 6 fig., Pl. 1-2, 1 Tab.

908 R. Macchiarelli, Prehistoric "Fish Eaters" along the eastern Arabian Coast: Dental Variation, Morphology and Oral Health in the Ra's al-Hamra Community (Qurum, Sultanate of Oman, 5th-4th Millennia B.C.), *in* American Journal of Physical Anthropology 78, 1989, pp. 575-594.

909 M. Uerpmann, Some remarks on the late Stone Age industries from the coastal area of Northern Oman, *in* Oman Studies, Papers on the archaeology and history of Oman [= Serie Orientale Roma 63 (P.M. Costa & M. Tosi, eds.)], Roma, 1989, pp. 169-177, 2 fig.

910 H.-P. Uerpmann, Prehistoric Oman, *in* PDO News [= Petroleum Development Oman News], Muscat, 1989-3, pp. 13-15, 6 fig.

911 L.E. Villiers-Petocz, Some Notes on the Lithic Collections of the Oman Department of Antiquities, *in* The Journal of Oman Studies 10, 1989, pp. 51-59, 1 fig., 1 Pl.

912 P. Biagi & R. Maggi, Archaeological Surveys along the Oman Coast: Preliminary Results of Five Years of Research (1983-1987), *in* South Asian Archaeology 1987 [= Proceedings of the Ninth International Conference of the Association of South Asian Archaeologists in Western

Europe held in the Fondazione Giorgio Cini, Venice (M. Taddei, ed.)], Rome, 1990, pp. 543-553, 7 fig.

913 R. MAGGI, The Chipped Flint Assemblage of RH 6 (Muscat, Sultanate of Oman). Some Considerations on Technological Aspects, *in* East and West 40/1-4, 1990, pp. 293-300, 5 fig.

914 R. MAGGI & H.G. GEBEL, A Preliminary Report on the Chipped Stone Industries of the Mid-Holocene Shell-Midden Communities of Ra's al-Hamra 5, Layer 1 (Muscat, Sultanate of Oman), *in* Rivista di Archeologia XIV, 1990, pp. 5-24, 16 fig.

915 H.-P. UERPMANN, Radiocarbon Dating of Shell Middens in the Sultanate of Oman, *in* PACT 29, 1990 [= Proceedings of the Second International Symposium 14C and Archeology, Groningen 1987 (W.G. Mook & H.T. Waterbolk, eds.)], Groningen, 1990, pp. 335-347, 3 fig.

916 V. CHARPENTIER, La fouille du campement préhistorique de Ra's al Junayz 37 (RJ 37) — Sultanat d' Oman, *in* Paléorient 17/1, 1991, pp. 127-141, 6 fig.

917 P. BIAGI & R. NISBET, Environmental history and plant exploitation at the aceramic sites of RH 5 and RH 6 near the mangrove swamp of Qurm (Muscat — Oman), *in* Les charbons de bois, les anciens écosystemes et le rôle de l'homme: 1992 (J.-L. Vernet, ed.) [= Bulletin de la Société Botanique de France 139], 1992, pp. 571-578.

918 M. UERPMANN, Structuring the Late Stone Age of Southeastern Arabia, *in* Arabian archaeology and epigraphy 3/2, 1992, pp. 65-109, 34 fig.

919 P. BIAGI, A radiocarbon chronology for the aceramic shell-middens of coastal Oman, *in* Arabian archaeology and epigraphy 5/1, 1994, pp. 17-31, 7 fig., 4 Tab.

920 P. BIAGI, An Early Palaeolithic site near Saiwan (Sultanate of Oman), *in* Arabian archaeology and epigraphy 5/2, 1994, pp. 81-88, 6 fig.

LATE 4TH MILLENNIUM — END 2ND MILLENNIUM B.C.

General studies

921 B. COMPAGNONI & M. TOSI, The Camel: its Distribution and State of Domestication in the Middle East during the Third Millennium B.C. in the light of the Finds from Shahr-i-Sokhta, *in* Approaches to Faunal Analysis in the Middle East (R.H. Meadow & M.A. Zeder, eds.) [= Peabody Museum Bulletin 2], 1978, pp. 91-104, 6 fig., 5 Tab.

922 W. DOSTAL, The Development of Bedouin Life in Arabia seen from archaeological material, *in* Sources for the History of Arabia, I [= Studies in the History of Arabia I], Riyadh, 1979, pp. 125-143, fig. 26, Pl. 60-72.

923 M.C. DE GRAEVE, Representations of Boats from the Periphery of Mesopotamia. The Old Babylonian Period, *in* M.C. De Graeve, The Ships of the Ancient Near East (c. 2000–500 B.C.): Seals of Failaka, Pl. VI (fig. 20-21) & Rock Carvings of large vessels at Jebel Jesasiya (Qatar), Pl. LIX (fig. 150) [= Orientalia Lovaniensia Analecta 7], Leuven, 1981, pp. 29-31 & 123.

924 D.T. POTTS, The Jamdat Nasr Culture Complex in the Arabian Gulf ca. 3000 B.C., *in* Pre-Islamic Arabia. Studies in the History of Arabia II [= Proceedings of the Second International Symposium on Studies in the History of Arabia 1399/1979], Riyadh, 1984, pp. 109-122, map 8, fig. 38.

925 A.A.H. BUSHIRI, The mythology of immortality, *in* Dilmun 13, 1985-'86, pp. 7-16, 10 fig.

926 A.A.H. BUSHIRI, The bull-game festival for Moon-God Nanna, *in* Dilmun 13, 1985-'86, pp. 47-52, 2 fig.

927 P. AMIET, Les communautés du Golfe Persique, I. La péninsule d'Oman, II. L'île de Bahrain, *in* P. Amiet, L'âge des échanges inter-iraniens. 3500–1700 avant J.-C., Paris, 1986, pp. 171-180.

928 C. EDENS, Bahrain and the Arabian Gulf during the second millennium B.C.: urban crisis and colonialism, *in* Bahrain through the ages, the Archaeology (Shaikha Haya Ali al-Khalifa & M. Rice, eds.), London, 1986, pp. 195-216.

929 D.T. POTTS, Eastern Arabia and the Oman Peninsula during the late Fourth and Early Third Millennium B.C., *in* Ǧamdat Naṣr Period or Regional Style? Papers given at a symposium held in Tübingen, November 1983 [= Beihefte zum Tübinger Atlas des Vorderen Orients, Reihe B],

(U. Finkbeiner & W. Röllig, eds.)], Wiesbaden, 1986, pp. 121-170, 7 fig., 3 Pl., 3 maps.

930 L. WERR al-GAILANI, Gulf (Dilmun)-style cylinder seals, *in* Proceedings of the Seminar for Arabian Studies 16 [= Proceedings of the 19th Seminar for Arabian Studies 1985], 1986, pp. 199-202, 5 fig.

931 M.-P. BAUDOT, "Steatite" Vessels in the Third Millennium in the Ancient Orient, *in* India and the Ancient World. History, Trade and Culture before A.D. 650 (G. Pollet, ed.) [= Orientalia Lovaniensia Analecta 25. Professor P.H.L. Eggermont Jubilee Volume], Leuven, 1987, pp. 1-32, IV Pl.

932 R.R. STIEGLITZ, Ebla and Dilmun, *in* Eblaitica: Essays on the Ebla Archives and Eblaite Language I (C.H. Gordon, G.A. Rendberg & N.H. Winter, eds.), Winona Lake, 1987, pp. 43-46.

933 S. CLEUZIOU, Dilmoun-Arabie (en marge de C.M. Piesinger: "The Legacy of Dilmun"), *in* L'Arabie et ses mers bordières I: Itinéraires et voisinages (J.-F. Salles, ed.) [= Travaux de la Maison de l'Orient 16], Lyon, 1988, pp. 27-58, 1 fig.

934 Y. CALVET, Le pays de Dilmoun au IIe millénaire: Découvertes récentes, *in* L'Arabie préislamique et son environnement historique et culturel [= Actes du Colloque de Strasbourg, 24–27 juin 1987 (T. Fahd, ed.)], Leiden, 1989, pp. 15-24, 2 fig.

935 S. CLEUZIOU & M. TOSI, The Southern Frontier of the ancient Near East, *in* South Asian Archaeology 1985 (K. Frifelt & P. Sørensen, eds.) [= Scandinavian Institute of Asian Studies Occasional Papers 4 — Papers from the Eighth International Conference of South Asian Archaeologists in Western Europe, Moesgaard, 1985], London & Riverdale, 1989, pp. 15-47, 12 fig., 6 maps.

936 S. MERY, Studies of Bronze Age Pottery in the Oman Peninsula: an archaeometrical perspective, *in* Oman Studies, Papers on the archaeology and history of Oman [= Serie Orientale Roma 63 (P.M. Costa & M. Tosi, eds.)], Roma, 1989, pp. 127-134, 1 fig., 3 Pl.

937 J. ZARINS, Pastoralism in Southwest Asia: the second millennium B.C., *in* The Walking Larder. Patterns of domestication, pastoralism and predation (J. Clutton-Brock, ed.), London, 1989, pp. 127-155, 10 fig., 2 Tab.

938 Ph. GOUIN, Rapes, jarres et faisselles. La production et l'exportation des produits laitiers dans l'Indus du 3e millénaire, *in* Paléorient 16/2, 1990, pp. 37-54, 7 fig., 2 Pl.

939 J. HÄSER, Soft-Stone Vessels of the 2nd Millennium B.C. in the Gulf Region, *in* Proceedings of the Seminar for Arabian Studies 20 [= Proceedings of the 23rd Seminar for Arabian Studies, held at London on 18th–20th July 1989], 1990, pp. 43-54, 5 fig.

940 E.C.L. DURING CASPERS, Further evidence for 'Central Asian' materials from the Arabian Gulf, *in* Journal of the Economic and Social History of the Orient XXXVII, 1994, pp. 33-53, 17 fig.

941 E.C.L. DURING CASPERS, Triangular stamp seals from the Arabian Gulf, once again, *in* Proceedings of the Seminar for Arabian Studies 24 [= Proceedings of the 27th Seminar for Arabian Studies held in London on 22–24 July 1993], 1994, pp. 97-114, XXVI Pl.

942 R. ZADOK, Elamites and other Peoples from Iran and the Persian Gulf Region in early Mesopotamian Sources, *in* Iran XXXII, 1994, pp. 31-51.

Kuwait

943 J.J. GLASSNER, Inscriptions cunéiformes de Failaka — Cuneiform Inscriptions from Failaka, *in* Failaka. Fouilles Françaises 1983 (J.-F. Salles, ed.) [= Travaux de la Maison de l'Orient 9], Lyon, 1984, pp. 31-50, fig. 4-23.

944 R. CIARLA, Bronze-Age Crafts at Failaka: Some Preliminary Observations on Stone Vase Fragments, *in* East and West 35/4, 1985, pp. 396-406, 11 fig.

945 D. BEYER, Les sceaux. The stamp-seals, *in* Failaka. Fouilles Françaises 1984-1985 (Y. Calvet & J.-F. Salles, eds.) [= Travaux de la Maison de l'Orient 12], Lyon, 1986, pp. 89-103, fig. 40-44.

946 Y. CALVET & J.J. GLASSNER, Un fragment de vase inscrit — An inscribed piece of vase, *in* Failaka. Fouilles Françaises 1984-1985 (Y. Calvet & J.-F. Salles, eds.) [= Travaux de la Maison de l'Orient 12], Lyon, 1986, pp. 105-106, fig. 45.

947 Y. CALVET & M. PIC, Un nouveau bâtiment de l' Age du Bronze sur le Tell F 6 — A new Bronze Age building on F 6, in Failaka. Fouilles Françaises 1984-1985 (Y. Calvet & J.-F. Salles, eds.) [= Travaux de la Maison de l'Orient 12], Lyon, 1986, pp. 13-87, fig. 4-39.

948 P. KJÆRUM, Architecture and settlement patterns in 2nd ml. Failaka, *in* Proceedings of the Seminar for Arabian Studies 16 [= Proceedings of the 19th Seminar for Arabian Studies 1985], 1986, pp. 77-88, 13 fig.

949 J. EIDEM, The Inscribed Pottery, *in* F. Højlund, Failaka/Dilmun. The Second Millennium Settlements 2: The Bronze Age Pottery [= Jutland Archaeological Society Publications XVII:2], Aarhus, 1987, pp. 179-180, fig. 718-720.

950 F. HØJLUND, Failaka/Dilmun. The Second Millennium Settlements. Vol. 2: The Bronze Age Pottery [= Jutland Archaeological Society Publications XVII:2], Aarhus, 1987, pp. 1-177, 717 fig.

951 A.M. POLLARD, Report on the analysis of Failaka glass, glazed pottery and faience, *in* F. Højlund, Failaka/Dilmun. The Second Millennium Settlements 2: The Bronze Age Pottery [= Jutland Archaeological Society Publications XVII:2], Aarhus, 1987, pp. 185-195, 5 Tab., 3 Appendix.

952 P. ROWLEY-CONWY, Remains of date (Phoenix dactilifera) from Failaka, Kuwait, *in* F. Højlund, Failaka/Dilmun. The Second Millennium Settlements 2: The Bronze Age Pottery [= Jutland Archaeological Society Publications XVII:2], Aarhus, 1987, pp. 181-183, fig. 721-725, Tab. 1-2.

953 Y. CALVET, Failaka and the Northern Part of Dilmun, *in* Proceedings of the Seminar for Arabian Studies 19 [= Proceedings of the 22nd Seminar for Arabian Studies 1988], 1989, pp. 5-11, 3 fig.

954 T. HOWARD-CARTER, Voyages of Votive Vessels in the Gulf, *in* DUMU-E2-DUB-BA-A Studies in Honor of Åke W. Sjöberg (H.Behrens, D. Loding & M.T. Roth, eds.) [= Occasional Publications of the Samuel Noach Kramer Fund 11], Philadelphia, 1989, pp. 253-266, 11 fig.

955 Y. CALVET & M. PIC, Un temple-tour de l'âge du Bronze à Failaka, *in* Failaka. Fouilles françaises 1986-1988 (Y. Calvet & J. Gachet, eds.) [= Travaux de la Maison de l'Orient 18], Lyon, 1990, pp. 103-122, 10 fig., Dépl. I-IV.

956 R. CIARLA, Fragments of Stone Vessels as a Base Material. Two Case studies: Failaka and Shahr-i Sokhta, *in* South Asian Archaeology 1987 [= Proceedings of the Ninth International Conference of the Association of South Asian Archaeologists in Western Europe held in the Fondazione Giorgio Cini, Venice (M. Taddei, ed.)], Rome, 1990, pp. 475-491, 14 fig.

957 J.J. GLASSNER, Inscriptions cunéiformes de Failaka: complément, *in* Failaka. Fouilles françaises 1986-1988 (Y. Calvet & J. Gachet, eds.) [= Travaux de la Maison de l'Orient 18], Lyon, 1990, pp. 123-124, 4 fig.

958 L. HURTEL & F. TALLON, Le métal en provenance du Tell F 6: description des objects et analyses, *in* Failaka. Fouilles françaises 1986-1988 (Y. Calvet & J. Gachet, eds.) [= Travaux de la Maison de l'Orient 18], Lyon, 1990, pp. 149-154, 3 fig.

959 A. LECLAIRE & G. QUERRE, Etude des terres, enduits et mortiers provenant de l'île de Failaka, *in* Failaka. Fouilles françaises 1986-1988 (Y. Calvet & J. Gachet, eds.) [= Travaux de la Maison de l'Orient 18], Lyon, 1990, pp. 155-166, 2 fig., 9 Pl., III Tab.

960 M. PIC, Quelques éléments de glyptique, *in* Failaka. Fouilles françaises 1986-1988 (Y. Calvet & J. Gachet, eds.) [= Travaux de la Maison de l'Orient 18], Lyon, 1990, pp. 125-140, 27 fig.

961 Y. CALVET, Un bâtiment de l'Age du Bronze à Failaka (Koweit), *in* Golf–Archäologie. Mesopotamien, Iran, Kuwait, Bahrain, Vereinigte Arabische Emirate und Oman (K. Schippmann, A. Herling & J.-F. Salles, eds.) [= Internationale Archäologie 6, Buch am Erlbach], Göttingen & Lyon, 1991, pp. 133-144, 6 fig.

Northeastern Arabia

962 J. ZARINS, A.S. al-MUGHANNUM & M. KAMAL, Excavations at Dhahran South. The Tumuli Field (208–91), 1403 A.H./1983. A Preliminary Report, *in* Atlal 8, 1984, pp. 25-54, 5 tab., Pl. 18-59.

963 B. FROHLICH & A.S. al-MUGHANNUM, Excavations of the Dhahran Burial Mounds 1404/1984, *in* Atlal 9, 1985, pp. 9-40, Pl. 1-29.

964 F. IPPOLITONI-STRIKA, The Tarut statue as a peripheral contribution to the knowledge of early Mesopotamian plastic art, *in* Bahrain through the ages, the Archaeology (Shaikha Haya Ali al-Khalifa & M. Rice, eds.), London, 1986, pp. 311-324, fig. 130-135.

965 A.S. al- MUGHANNUM & J. WARWICK, Excavations of the Dhahran Burial Mounds, Third Season, 1405/1985-1986, *in* Atlal 10, 1986, pp. 9-27, Pl. 1-28.

966 W. LANCASTER, The skeletal material from the Dhahran South Burial Mound Excavations; 1975 and 1983 to 1986, *in* Atlal 11, 1988, pp. 101-106, 2 Tab.

967 A.S. al-MUGHANNUM, Excavation of the Dhahran Burial Mounds, Fourth Season, 1406/1986, *in* Atlal 11, 1988, pp. 9-28, Pl. 1-10.

968 J. ZARINS, Eastern Saudi Arabia and External Relations: Selected Ceramic, Steatite, and Textual Evidence: 3500–1900 BC, *in* South Asian Archaeology 1985 (K. Frifelt & P. Sørensen, eds.) [= Scandinavian Institute of Asian Studies Occasional Papers 4 — Papers from the Eighth International Conference of South Asian Archaeologists in Western Europe, Moesgaard, 1985], London & Riverdale, 1989, pp. 74-103, 16 fig., 1 Tab.

Bahrain

969 E.C.L. DURING CASPERS, Review of S. Cleuziou, P. Lombard & J.-F. Salles: Fouilles à Umm Jidr (Bahrain), *in* Bibliotheca Orientalis XL/3-4, 1983, pp. 483-486.

970 K. Frifelt, Burial Mounds near Ali excavated by the Danish Expedition, *in* Dilmun 12, 1984-'85, pp. 11-14.

971 B. Doe, Masonry of the Dilmun Temple at Barbar, *in* Proceedings of the Seminar for Arabian Studies 15 [= Proceedings of the 18th Seminar for Arabian Studies 1984], 1985, pp. 35-40, 5 fig.

972 H.H. Andersen, The Barbar Temple Re-excavated, *in* Dilmun 13, 1985-'86, pp. 53-60, 7 fig.

973 H.H. Andersen, The Barbar Temple: stratigraphy, architecture and interpretation, *in* Bahrain through the ages, the Archaeology (Shaikha Haya Ali al-Khalifa & M. Rice, eds.), London, 1986, pp. 166-177, fig. 35-43.

974 G. Bibby, The origins of the Dilmun Civilization, *in* Bahrain through the ages, the Archaeology (Shaikha Haya Ali al-Khalifa & M. Rice, eds.), London, 1986, pp. 108-115, fig. 25-29.

975 B. Doe, The Barbar Temple site in Bahrain: conservation and presentation, *in* Bahrain through the ages, the Archaeology (Shaikha Haya Ali al-Khalifa & M. Rice, eds.), London, 1986, pp. 480-484, fig. 166-168.

976 B. Doe, The Barbar Temple: the masonry, *in* Bahrain through the ages, the Archaeology (Shaikha Haya Ali al-Khalifa & M. Rice, eds.), London, 1986, pp. 186-191, fig. 49-54.

977 K. Frifelt, Burial mounds near Ali excavated by the Danish Expedition, *in* Bahrain through the ages, the Archaeology (Shaikha Haya Ali al-Khalifa & M. Rice, eds.), London, 1986, pp. 125-134, fig. 30-34.

978 B. Frohlich, The human biological history of the Early Bronze Age population in Bahrain, *in* Bahrain through the ages, the Archaeology (Shaikha Haya Ali al-Khalifa & M. Rice, eds.), London, 1986, pp. 47-63, fig. 12-18, 6 Tab.

979 F. Højlund, The chronology of City II and III at Qal'at al-Bahrain, *in* Bahrain through the ages, the Archaeology (Shaikha Haya Ali al-Khalifa & M. Rice, eds.), London, 1986, pp. 217-224, fig. 55-62.

980 H.A. al-Khalifa, The shell seals of Bahrain, *in* Bahrain through the ages, the Archaeology (Shaikha Haya Ali al-Khalifa & M. Rice, eds.), London, 1986, pp. 251-261, fig. 69-84.

981 A. Lowe, Bronze Age Burial Mounds on Bahrain, *in* Iraq 48, 1986, pp. 73-84, 12 fig.

982 P. Mortensen, The Barbar Temple: its chronology and foreign relations reconsidered, *in* Bahrain through the ages, the Archaeology (Shaikha Haya Ali al-Khalifa & M. Rice, eds.), London, 1986, pp. 178-185, fig. 44-48.

983 B. Frohlich, D.J. Ortner & H.A. al-Khalifa, Human Disease in the Ancient Middle East, *in* Dilmun 14, 1987-'88, pp. 61-73, 5 fig.

984 S. Cleuziou, The Early Dilmun Period (Third and Early Second Millennium BC.), *in* Bahrain National Museum. Archaeological Collections I. A Selection of Pre-Islamic Antiquities from Excavations 1954-1975 (P. Lombard & M. Kervran, eds.), Manama, 1989, pp. 9-36, fig. 1-61.

985 S. Cleuziou, The Middle Dilmun Period (1700–1200 BC.), *in* Bahrain National Museum. Archaeological Collections I. A Selection of Pre-Islamic Antiquities from Excavations 1954-1975 (P. Lombard & M. Kervran, eds.), Manama, 1989, pp. 37-47, fig. 62-86.

986 E.C.L. During Caspers, Mackay's Ivory Figurine from Tumulus 12 at 'Ali, Bahrain, *in* Iranica Antiqua XXIV, 1989, pp. 159-174, 1 Pl.

987 F. Højlund, The Formation of the Dilmun State and the Amorite Tribes, *in* Proceedings of the Seminar for Arabian Studies 19 [= Proceedings of the 22nd Seminar for Arabian Studies 1988], 1989, pp. 45-59, 1 fig.

988 F. Højlund, Date Honey Production of Dilmun in the Mid 2nd Millennium B.C.: Steps in the technological evolution of the Madbasa, *in* Paléorient 16/1, 1990, pp. 77-86, 10 fig.

989 H. Crawford, Seals from the first season's excavation at Saar, Bahrain, *in* Cambridge Archaeological Journal 1:2, 1991, pp. 255-262, 14 fig.

990 E.C.L. During Caspers, A Harappan Bronze found in the Jefferson Tumulus on Bahrain. The Arabian Gulf and South Asia at the turn of the third millennium B.C., *in* Golf–Archäologie. Mesopotamien, Iran, Kuwait, Bahrain, Vereinigte Arabische Emirate und Oman (K. Schippmann, A. Herling & J.-F. Salles, eds.) [= Internationale Archäologie 6, Buch am Erlbach], Göttingen & Lyon, 1991, pp. 159-174, 1 fig., Pl. I-II.

991 R.G. Killick, H.E.W. Crawford, K. Flavin, H. Ginger, A. Lupton, C. MacLaughlin, R. Montague, J.A. Moon & M.A. Woodburn, London-Bahrain Archaeological Expedition: 1990 excavations at Saar, *in* Arabian archaeology and epigraphy 2/2, 1991, pp. 107-137, 22 fig.

992 R.J. al-Hashmi, Dilmun through the Cuneiforms, *in* Dilmun 15, 1991-'92, pp. 12-16.

993 F. Højlund, Holy Architecture in Bronze Age Bahrain, *in* Dilmun 15, 1991-'92, pp. 73-79, 3 fig.

994 A.A. Soweileh, A Typology of Dilmun Burial Mounds, *in* Dilmun 15, 1991-'92, pp. 23-66, var. fig.

995 H. Crawford, London-Bahrain Archaeological Expedition: excavations at Saar 1991, *in* Arabian archaeology and epigraphy 4/1, 1993, pp. 1-19, 14 fig.

996 F. Højlund, The ethnic composition of the population of Dilmun, *in* Proceedings of the Seminar for Arabian Studies 23 [= Proceedings of the 26th Seminar for Arabian Studies, held at Manchester 1992], 1993, pp. 1-8, 1 fig.

997 M. NESBITT, Archaeological evidence for early Dilmun diet at Saar, Bahrain, *in* Arabian archaeology and epigraphy 4/1, 1993, pp. 20-47, 5 fig.

998 M. UERPMANN, Animal remains from Qala'at Al-Bahrain, a preliminary report, *in* Archaeozoology of the Near East: Proceedings of the first international symposium on the archaeozoology of southwestern Asia and adjacent areas (H. Buitenhuis & A.T. Clason, eds.), Leiden, 1993, pp. 60-66.

999 B.E. DENTON, Pottery, cylinder seals, and stone vessels from the cemeteries of al-Hajjar, al-Maqsha and Hamad Town on Bahrain, *in* Arabian archaeology and epigraphy 5/2, 1994, pp. 121-151, 36 fig.

1000 K.M. DOBNEY & D. JAQUES, Preliminary report on the animal bones from Saar, *in* Arabian archaeology and epigraphy 5/2, 1994, pp. 106-120, 21 fig., 3 Tab.

1001 J. EIDEM, Cuneiform inscriptions, *in* F. Højlund & H.H. Andersen, Qala'at al-Bahrain, Vol. 1, The Northern City Wall and the Islamic Fortress. The Carlsberg Foundation's Gulf Project (P. Mortensen, ed.) [= Jutland Archaeological Society Publications XXX:1], Aarhus, 1994, pp. 300-303, fig. 1714-1715.

1002 R. GALE, Charcoal from an Early Dilmun settlement at Saar, Bahrain, *in* Arabian archaeology and epigraphy 5/4, 1994, pp. 229-235, 2 Tab.

1003 A. HAUPTMANN, Analysis of copper ingots, *in* F. Højlund & H.H. Andersen, Qala'at al-Bahrain, Vol. 1, The Northern City Wall and the Islamic Fortress. The Carlsberg Foundation's Gulf Project (P. Mortensen, ed.) [= Jutland Archaeological Society Publications XXX:1], Aarhus, 1994, p. 381, fig. 1876-1880.

1004 M. HEINZ, Die Keramik aus Saar/Bahrain. Ergebnisse der Kampagnen 1990/1991 und 1991/1992, *in* Baghdader Mitteilungen 25, 1994, pp. 119-307, 5 Abb., 530 fig., 19 Tab., Taf. 4-6.

1005 A. HERLING, Excavations at Karranah Mound I, Bahrain. A preliminary report, *in* Iranica Antiqua XXIX [= Festschrift K. Schippmann I], 1994, pp. 225-239, 8 fig.

1006 P. KJÆRUM, Stamp-seals, seal impressions and seal blanks, *in* F. Højlund & H.H. Andersen, Qala'at al-Bahrain, Vol. 1, The Northern City Wall and the Islamic Fortress. The Carlsberg Foundation's Gulf Project (P. Mortensen, ed.) [= Jutland Archaeological Society Publications XXX:1], Aarhus, 1994, pp. 319-350, fig. 1723-1758.

1007 P. NORTHOVER, Analysis of crucible sherds, *in* F. Højlund & H.H. Andersen, Qala'at al-Bahrain, Vol. 1, The Northern City Wall and the Islamic Fortress. The Carlsberg Foundation's Gulf Project (P. Mortensen, ed.) [= Jutland Archaeological Society Publications XXX:1], Aarhus, 1994, pp. 374-377, fig. 1836-1853.

1008 A. Parpola, An analytical catalogue of the Indus inscriptions from the Near East, *in* F. Højlund & H.H. Andersen, Qala'at al-Bahrain, Vol. 1, The Northern City Wall and the Islamic Fortress. The Carlsberg Foundation's Gulf Project (P. Mortensen, ed.) [= Jutland Archaeological Society Publications XXX:1], Aarhus, 1994, pp. 304-315, fig. 1716-1720.

1009 M. Uerpmann & H.-P. Uerpmann, Animal bone finds from Excavation 520 at Qala'at al-Bahrain, *in* F. Højlund & H.H. Andersen, Qala'at al-Bahrain, Vol. 1, The Northern City Wall and the Islamic Fortress. The Carlsberg Foundation's Gulf Project (P. Mortensen, ed.) [= Jutland Archaeological Society Publications XXX:1], Aarhus, 1994, pp. 417-444, fig. 2076-2086, 18 Tab.

1010 W. Van Neer & M. Uerpmann, Fish remains from Excavation 520 at Qala'at al-Bahrain, *in* F. Højlund & H.H. Andersen, Qala'at al-Bahrain, Vol. 1, The Northern City Wall and the Islamic Fortress. The Carlsberg Foundation's Gulf Project (P. Mortensen, ed.) [= Jutland Archaeological Society Publications XXX:1], Aarhus, 1994, pp. 445-454, fig. 2087-2095, 2 Tab.

1011 C. Velde, Die steinernen Türme. Gedanken zum Aussehen der bronzezeitlichen Gräber und zur Struktur der Friedhöfe auf Bahrain, *in* Iranica Antiqua XXIX [= Festschrift K. Schippmann I], 1994, pp. 63-82, 4 Abb.

1012 M.A. Woodburn & H.E.W. Crawford, London-Bahrain Archaeological Expedition: 1991-2 excavations at Saar, *in* Arabian archaeology and epigraphy 5/2, 1994, pp. 89-105, 21 fig.

1013 E. Glover, Molluscan evidence for diet and environment at Saar in the early second millennium BC, *in* Arabian archaeology and epigraphy 6/3, 1995, pp. 157-179, 6 fig., 9 Tab.

1014 M. Heinz, Bahrain als Handelsdrehscheibe im 3. und 2. Jt. v. Chr., *in* Beiträge zur Kulturgeschichte Vorderasiens. Festschrift für Rainer Michael Boehmer (U. Finkbeiner, R. Dittmann & H. Hauptmann, Hrsg.), Mainz, 1995, pp. 237-255, 4 Abb., Taf. 21-29.

1015 F. Højlund, Bitumen-coated basketry in Bahraini burials, *in* Arabian archaeology and epigraphy 6/2, 1995, pp. 100-102, 4 fig.

1016 F. Højlund, Evidence for a Kassite temple at Qala'at al-Bahrain?, *in* Arabian archaeology and epigraphy 6/3, 1995, pp. 199-202, 6 fig.

1017 J. Littleton, Empty tombs? The taphonomy of burials on Bahrain, *in* Arabian archaeology and epigraphy 6/1, 1995, pp. 5-14, 4 Tab.

1018 J. Moon & R. Killick, A Dilmun residence on Bahrain, *in* Beiträge zur Kulturgeschichte Vorderasiens. Festschrift für Rainer Michael Boehmer (U. Finkbeiner, R. Dittmann & H. Hauptmann, Hrsg.), Mainz, 1995, pp. 413-438, 1 fig., Tab., Pl. 33 d-g.

1019 J. MOON, S. FARID, A. HICKS, M. HICKS & J. KIELY, with notes by B. IRVING, W. MATTHEWS & CH. FRENCH, London-Bahrain Archaeological Expedition excavations at Saar: 1993 season, *in* Arabian archaeology and epigraphy 6/3, 1995, pp. 139-156, 18 fig., 1 Tab.

1020 A.A. SOWEILEH, A Typology of Dilmun Burial Mounds, *in* The Archaeology of Death in the Ancient Near East (St. Campbell & A. Green, eds.) [= Oxbow Monograph 51], Oxford, 1995, pp. 196-198.

Qatar

1021 C.M. EDENS, A late Second Millennium B.C. Purple Dye Industry in Qatar (Arabian Gulf). Archaeological and Historical Interpretations, [= Dissertation Abstracts International section A. The Humanities and Social Sciences, U.S.A., Harvard, 1987, 784 p.], 48/11, 1988, p. 2915.

United Arab Emirates

1022 S. MERY, Wadi Suq fine wares from Shimal and Hili sites (United Arab Emirates). A technological and provenience analysis, *in* Golf–Archäologie. Mesopotamien, Iran, Kuwait, Bahrain, Vereinigte Arabische Emirate und Oman (K. Schippmann, A. Herling & J.-F. Salles, eds.) [= Internationale Archäologie 6, Buch am Erlbach], Göttingen & Lyon, 1991, pp. 245-255, 4 fig.

Abu Dhabi

1023 S. CLEUZIOU & B. VOGT, Tomb A at Hili North (United Arab Emirates) and Its Material Connections to Southeast Iran and the Greater Indus Valley, *in* South Asian Archaeology 1983. Papers from the Seventh International Conference of the Association of South Asian Archaeologists in Western Europe, held in the Musées Royaux d'Art et d'Histoire, Brussels (J. Schotsmans & M. Taddei, eds.), Naples, 1985, pp. 249-277, 10 fig.

1024 M. el-NAJJAR, An Anthropological Study on Skeletal Remains from Tomb A Hili North, *in* Archaeology in the United Arab Emirates IV, 1985, pp. 38-43, 1 Tab., Pl. 30-34.

1025 W.Y. al-TIKRITI, The Archaeological Investigations on Ghanadha Island 1982-1984: Further Evidence for the Coastal Umm an-Nar Culture, *in* Archaeology in the United Arab Emirates IV, 1985, pp. 9-19, Pl. 1-20.

1026 B. VOGT, The Umm an-Nar Tomb A at Hili North: A preliminary report on three seasons of excavations, 1982-1984, *in* Archaeology in the United Arab Emirates IV, al-Ain, 1985, pp. 20-37, Pl. 21-29.

1027 M.J. BLACKMAN, S. MERY & R.P. WRIGHT, Production and Exchange of Ceramics on the Oman Peninsula from the Perspective of Hili, *in* Journal of Field Archaeology 16/1, 1989, pp. 61-77, 10 fig., 2 Tab.

1028 K. FRIFELT, A third millennium kiln from the Oman Peninsula, *in* Arabian archaeology and epigraphy 1/1, 1990, pp. 4-15, 17 fig.

1029 K. FRIFELT, The Island of Umm an-Nar. Vol. I: Third Millennium Graves. The Carlsberg Foundation's Gulf Project (P. Mortensen, ed.) [= Jutland Archaeological Society Publications XXVI:1], Aarhus, 1991, 162 p., 254 fig.

1030 E. HOCH, Bones of Small Animals in Grave I, *in* K. Frifelt, The Island of Umm an-Nar. Vol. I: Third Millennium Graves. The Carlsberg Foundation's Gulf Project (P. Mortensen, ed.) [= Jutland Archaeological Society Publications XXVI:1], Aarhus, 1991, pp. 180-183.

1031 M. KUNTER, Die menschlichen Skelettreste aus den Gräbern von Umm an-Nar, Abu Dhabi, U.A.E. (3. Jt. v. Chr.), *in* K. Frifelt, The Island of Umm an-Nar. Vol. I: Third Millennium Graves. The Carlsberg Foundation's Gulf Project (P. Mortensen, ed.) [= Jutland Archaeological Society Publications XXVI:1], Aarhus, 1991, pp. 163-179, 9 Pl., 4 Tab.

1032 D.S. REESE, Shells from the Umm an-Nar and Hafit Graves, Abu Dhabi, *in* K. Frifelt, The Island of Umm an-Nar. Vol. I: Third Millennium Graves. The Carlsberg Foundation's Gulf Project (P. Mortensen, ed.) [= Jutland Archaeological Society Publications XXVI:1], Aarhus, 1991, pp. 184-186, fig. 255-257.

1033 K.W. ALT, W. VACH, K. FRIFELT & M. KUNTER, Familienanalyse in kupferzeitlichen Kollektivgräbern aus Umm an-Nar, Abu Dhabi, *in* Arabian archaeology and epigraphy 6/2, 1995, pp. 65-80, 2 Abb., 7 Tab.

1034 K. FRIFELT, The Island of Umm an-Nar. Vol. II: Third Millennium Settlement. The Carlsberg Foundation's Gulf Project [= Jutland Archaeological Society Publications XXVI:2], Aarhus, 1995, 245 p., 344 ill., 12 Tab., 5 Pl.

1035 A. HAUPTMANN, Chemische Zusammensetzung von Metallobjekten aus der Siedlung von Umm an-Nar, *in* K. Frifelt, The Island of Umm an-Nar. Vol. II: Third Millennium Settlement. The Carlsberg Foundation's Gulf

Project [= Jutland Archaeological Society Publications XXVI:2], Aarhus, 1995, pp. 246-248, 1 Abb., 1 Tab.

1036 E. HOCH, Animal Bones from the Umm an-Nar Settlement, *in* K. Frifelt, The Island of Umm an-Nar. Vol. II: Third Millennium Settlement. The Carlsberg Foundation's Gulf Project [= Jutland Archaeological Society Publications XXVI:2], Aarhus, 1995, pp. 249-256, II Pl.

1037 G. WILLCOX, Some Plant Impressions from Umm an-Nar Island, *in* K. Frifelt, The Island of Umm an-Nar. Vol. II: Third Millennium Settlement. The Carlsberg Foundation's Gulf Project [= Jutland Archaeological Society Publications XXVI:2], Aarhus, 1995, pp. 257-259, ill.

Sharjah

1038 P. HELLYER, Kalba Archaeology, *in* Tribulus. Bulletin of the Emirates Natural History Group 3/1, 1993, p. 25.

1039 J. BENTON, Excavations at Jebel Al Emalah, *in* Tribulus. Bulletin of the Emirates Natural History Group 4/1, 1994, pp. 12-13, 1 fig.

Ajman

1040 W.Y. al-TIKRITI, Umm An-Nar Culture in the Northern Emirates: third millennium BC tombs at Ajman, *in* Archaeology in the United Arab Emirates V, 1989, pp. 89-99, Pl. 35B-58.

1041 E. HAERINCK, The rectangular Umm an-Nar-period Grave at Mowaihat (Emirate of Ajman, United Arab Emirates), *in* Gentse Bijdragen tot de Kunstgeschiedenis en Oudheidkunde XXIX (1990-1991), Gent, 1991, pp. 1-30, 9 fig., IX Pl.

1042 P. HELLYER, Ajman Archaeology, *in* Tribulus. Bulletin of the Emirates Natural History Group 1/1, 1991, p. 25.

Umm al-Qaiwain

1043 D.T. POTTS, A new Bactrian find from southeastern Arabia, *in* Antiquity 67, n°. 256, September 1993, pp. 591-596, 3 fig.

1044 W.J. READE & D.T. POTTS, New evidence for late Third Millennium Linen from Tell Abraq, Umm al-Qaiwain, U.A.E., *in* Paléorient 19/2, 1993, pp. 99-106, 1 Pl.

Ras al-Khaimah

1045 B. DE CARDI, Harappan finds in a tomb at Ras al-Khaimah, U.A.E., *in* Proceedings of the Seminar for Arabian Studies 16 [= Proceedings of the 19th Seminar for Arabian Studies 1985], 1986, pp. 23-24, 1 fig.

1046 B. DE CARDI, The Grave-goods from Shimal Tomb 6 in Ras al-Khaimah, *in* Araby the Blest. Studies in Arabian Archaeology (D.T. Potts, ed.), Margaret Golding in Memoriam [= Carsten Niebuhr Institute Publications 7], Copenhagen, 1988, pp. 44-71, 14 fig.

1047 B. DE CARDI, Harappan Finds from Tomb 6 at Shimal, Ras al-Khaimah, U.A.E., *in* South Asian Archaeology 1985 (K. Frifelt & P. Sørensen, eds.) [= Scandinavian Institute of Asian Studies Occasional Papers 4 — Papers from the Eighth International Conference of South Asian Archaeologists in Western Europe, Moesgaard, 1985], London & Riverdale, 1989, pp. 9-13, 2 fig.

1048 G. GRUPE & H. SCHUTKOWSKI, Dietary shift during the 2nd millennium BC in prehistoric Shimal, Oman Peninsula, *in* Paléorient 15/2, 1989, pp. 77-84, 2 fig., 3 Tab.

1049 J.-M. KÄSTNER, Vorbericht über zwei untersuchte Kollektivgräber in Dhayah (Ras al-Khaimah, U.A.E.), *in* Gedenkschrift für Jürgen Driehaus (F.M. Andraschko & W.-R. Teegen, eds.), Mainz, 1990, pp. 339-346, Taf. 40, 6 Abb.

1050 C. VELDE, Preliminary Remarks on the Settlement Pottery in Shimal (Ras al-Khaimah, U.A.E.), *in* Gedenkschrift für Jürgen Driehaus (F.M. Andraschko & W.-R. Teegen, eds.), Mainz, 1990, pp. 357-378, 17 fig.

1051 J.-M. KÄSTNER, Some preliminary remarks concerning two recently excavated tombs in Dhayah / Ras al-Khaimah, *in* Golf–Archäologie. Mesopotamien, Iran, Kuwait, Bahrain, Vereinigte Arabische Emirate und Oman (K. Schippmann, A. Herling & J.-F. Salles, eds.) [= Internationale Archäologie 6, Buch am Erlbach], Göttingen & Lyon, 1991, pp. 233-244, 7 fig.

1052 J. SCHMIDT, Report on geomorphological research at Shimal, Emirate of Ras al-Khaimah, *in* Golf–Archäologie. Mesopotamien, Iran, Kuwait, Bahrain, Vereinigte Arabische Emirate und Oman (K. Schippmann, A. Herling & J.-F. Salles, eds.) [= Internationale Archäologie 6, Buch am Erlbach], Göttingen & Lyon, 1991, pp. 257-264, 6 fig., 1 Tab.

1053 C. VELDE, Preliminary remarks on the settlement pottery in Shimal, *in* Golf–Archäologie. Mesopotamien, Iran, Kuwait, Bahrain, Vereinigte Arabische Emirate und Oman (K. Schippmann, A. Herling & J.-F. Salles, eds.) [= Internationale Archäologie 6, Buch am Erlbach], Göttingen & Lyon, 1991, pp. 265-288, 17 fig.

1054 A. VON DEN DRIESCH, Viehhaltung, Jagd und Fischfang in der bronzezeitlichen Siedlung von Shimal bei Ras al-Khaimah/U.A.E., *in* Beiträge zur Altorientalischen Archäologie und Altertumskunde. Festschrift für Barthel Hrouda zum 65. Geburtstag (P. Calmeyer, K. Hecker, L. Jacob-Rost & C.B.F. Walker, Hrsg.), Wiesbaden, 1994, pp. 73-85, 2 Tab., 2 Diagr., Taf. X-XI.

1055 D. KENNET & C. VELDE, Third and early second-millennium occupation at Nud Ziba, Khatt (U.A.E.), *in* Arabian archaeology and epigraphy 6/2, 1995, pp. 81-99, 15 fig.

1056 P. KRACHT, Ras al-Khaimah (Vereinigte Arabische Emirate), *in* Die Aktivitäten des Deutschen Archäologischen Instituts während der Grabungssaison 1994, *in* Antike Welt, 26. Jrg., Nr. 4, 1995, p. 295, Abb. 20.

Fujairah

1057 W.Y. al-TIKRITI, The Excavations at Bidya, Fujairah: the 3rd and 2nd millennia B.C. culture, *in* Archaeology in the United Arab Emirates V, 1989, pp. 101-114, Pl. 59-97.

Oman

1058 K. FRIFELT, Further Evidence of the Third Millennium B.C. Town at Bat in Oman, *in* The Journal of Oman Studies 7, 1985, pp. 89-104, 8 fig., 4 Pl.

1059 K. HØJGAARD, SEM (Scanning Electron Microscopic) Examination of Teeth from the Third Millennium B.C. Excavated in Wadi Jizzi and Hafit, *in* South Asian Archaeology 1983. Papers from the Seventh International Conference of the Association of South Asian Archaeologists in Western Europe, held in the Musées Royaux d'Art et d'Histoire, Brussels (J. Schotsmans & M. Taddei, eds.), Naples, 1985, pp. 151-156, 2 fig.

1060 A. HAUPTMANN, Kupfer und Bronzen der südostarabischen Halbinsel, *in* Der Anschnitt 39/5-6, 1987, pp. 209-218, 10 fig., 3 Tab.

1061 H.G. GEBEL, Südostarabien. Prähistorische Besiedlung, *in* Tübinger Atlas des Vorderen Orients, Karten BI 8.3.2 (Frühbronzezeit der Omanischen Halbinsel), Wiesbaden, 1988.

1062 J.B. BACQUART & S. CLEUZIOU, Preliminary Study on bitumen pieces found at RJ-2, *in* The Joint Hadd Project. Summary Report on the Second Season. November 1986–January 1987 (S. Cleuziou & M. Tosi, eds.), 1989, pp. 51-55, fig. 41-45.

1063 R.H. BRUNSWIG JR., Cultural History, Environment and Economy as seen from an Umm an-Nar Settlement: Evidence from Test Excavations at Bat,

Oman, 1977-78, *in* The Journal of Oman Studies 10, 1989, pp. 9-50, 22 fig., 4 Pl.

1064 S. Cleuziou, The chronology of protohistoric Oman as seen from Hili, *in* Oman Studies, Papers on the archaeology and history of Oman [= Serie Orientale Roma 63 (P.M. Costa & M. Tosi, eds.)], Roma, 1989, pp. 47-78, 8 fig.

1065 E.C.L. During Caspers, Some Remarks on Oman, *in* Proceedings of the Seminar for Arabian Studies 19 [= Proceedings of the 22nd Seminar for Arabian Studies 1988], 1989, pp. 13-31, 13 fig.

1066 P. Gentelle & K. Frifelt, About the distribution of third millennium graves and settlements in the Ibri area of Oman, *in* Oman Studies, Papers on the archaeology and history of Oman [= Serie Orientale Roma 63 (P.M. Costa & M. Tosi, eds.)], Roma, 1989, pp. 119-126, 1 map.

1067 S. Mery, The Soundings North of RJ-2, *in* The Joint Hadd Project. Summary Report on the Second Season. November 1986–January 1987 (S. Cleuziou & M. Tosi, eds.), 1989, pp. 27-29, fig. 24-26.

1068 S. Mery, Ceramics from RJ-2, *in* The Joint Hadd Project. Summary Report on the Second Season. November 1986–January 1987 (S. Cleuziou & M. Tosi, eds.), 1989, pp. 41-47, fig. 34-38.

1069 J. Reade & S. Mery, A Bronze Age Site at Ra's al-Hadd, *in* The Joint Hadd Project. Summary Report on the Second Season. November 1986–January 1987 (S. Cleuziou & M. Tosi, eds.), 1989, pp. 75-77, fig. 60-62.

1070 G. Santini, Preliminary Report on the Second Field Season at RJ-6, *in* The Joint Hadd Project. Summary Report on the Second Season. November 1986–January 1987 (S. Cleuziou & M. Tosi, eds.), 1989, pp. 33-40, fig. 28-33.

1071 A.A.B. al-Shanfari & G. Weisgerber, A late Bronze Age warrior burial from Nizwa (Oman), *in* Oman Studies, Papers on the archaeology and history of Oman [= Serie Orientale Roma 63 (P.M. Costa & M. Tosi, eds.)], Roma, 1989, pp. 17-30, 4 fig., 5 Pl.

1072 Anonymus, Other operations carried out in the Ra's al-Junayz embayment, *in* The Joint Hadd Project. Summary Report on the Third Season. October 1987–February 1988 (S. Cleuziou, J. Reade & M. Tosi, eds.), 1990, pp. 28-30, fig. 25-28.

1073 P. Biagi, Excavations at site RJ-1, structure 5. Autumn 1987 Campaign, *in* The Joint Hadd Project. Summary Report on the Third Season. October 1987–February 1988 (S. Cleuziou, J. Reade & M. Tosi, eds.), 1990, pp. 4-10, fig. 1-6.

1074 L. Bondioli & A. Lazzari, Some Aspects of Data Treatment of the Shahr-i Sokhta, Ra's al-Junayz and Moenjo-daro Records, *in* South Asian

Archaeology 1987 [= Proceedings of the Ninth International Conference of the Association of South Asian Archaeologists in Western Europe held in the Fondazione Giorgio Cini, Venice (M. Taddei, ed.)], Rome, 1990, pp. 377-390, 5 fig.

1075 K. FRIFELT, Investigations at Bat, Oman, 1989, *in* The Arabian Gulf Gazetteer I,1 (E.C.L. During Caspers, ed.), Leiden, 1990, p. 20, 1 fig.

1076 S. MERY, Origine et production des récipients de terre cuite dans la péninsule d'Oman à l'Age du Bronze, *in* Paléorient 17/2, 1991, pp. 51-78, 12 fig., 6 Tab.

1077 P. YULE, Neue archäologische Entdeckungen am Persisch-Arabischen Golf, *in* Antike Welt 23/4, 1992, pp. 274-279, 14 Abb.

1078 D.T. POTTS, Soft-stone from Oman and Eastern Iran in Cuneiform Sources?, *in* Res Orientales V [Circulation des monnaies, des marchandises et des biens], 1993, pp. 9-13, 1 carte.

1079 A.A.B. al-SHANFARI, Tower Tombs of the Eastern Hajjar, *in* PDO News [= Petroleum Development Oman News], Muscat, 1993-1, pp. 12-16, var. fig.

1080 V. CHARPENTIER, A specialized production at regional scale in Bronze Age Arabia: shell rings from Ra's al-Junayz area (Sultanate of Oman), *in* South Asian Archaeology 1993. Proceedings of the Twelfth International Conference of the European Association of South Asian Archaeologists held in Helsinki University 5–9 July 1993 (A. Parpola & P. Koskikallio, eds.) [= Annales Academiae Scientiarum Fennicae, ser. B., Tom. 271], Vol. 1, Helsinki, 1994, pp. 157-170, 4 fig.

1081 S. CLEUZIOU & M. TOSI, Black boats of Magan: some thoughts on Bronze Age water transport in Oman and beyond from the impressed bitumen slabs of Ra's al-Junayz, *in* South Asian Archaeology 1993. Proceedings of the Twelfth International Conference of the European Association of South Asian Archaeologists held in Helsinki University 5–9 July 1993 (A. Parpola & P. Koskikallio, eds.) [= Annales Academiae Scientiarum Fennicae, ser. B., Tom. 271], Vol. 2, Helsinki, 1994, pp. 745-761, 8 fig., 1 Tab.

1082 J. ORCHARD, Third Millennium Oasis Towns and Environmental Constraints on Settlement in the al-Hajar region. Part I: The al-Hajar Oasis Towns, *in* Iraq LVI, 1994, pp. 63-88, 12 fig.

1083 G. STANGER, Third Millennium Oasis Towns and Environmental Constraints on Settlement in the al-Hajar region. Part II: Environmental factors affecting early settlement south of the Jabal al-Akhdar, Oman, *in* Iraq LVI, 1994, pp. 89-100, fig. 12-18.

1084 P. YULE, Grabtürme des dritten vorchristlichen Jahrtausends am Golf von Oman, *in* Spektrum der Wissenschaft, November 1994, pp. 22-24, 3 Abb.

1085 J. ORCHARD, The origins of agricultural settlement in the al-Hajar region, *in* Iraq LVII, 1995, pp. 145-158, 4 fig.

Studies on Dilmun, Magan and Meluhha, and on trade and trade mechanism

1086 B. MEISSNER, Tilmun, *in* Orientalistische Literaturzeitung 20/7, 1917, pp. 201-203.

1087 F. HOMMEL, Arabien: Die Gebirge von Magan und Meluch, *in* Handbuch der Altertumswissenschaft: Ethnologie und Geographie des Alten Orients, München, 1926, pp. 539-546.

1088 J. DE MORGAN, La préhistoire orientale, Tome III, Paris, 1927, pp. 116 & 120-123.

1089 E. UNGER, Tilmun, *in* Reallexikon der Vorgeschichte 13, 1929, pp. 312-313.

1090 F. SCHOLLMEYER, Enzag und Miskilak, die Götter von Tilmun, *in* Die Welt des Orients I/5, 1950, p. 355.

1091 L. CASSON, International Trade begins, *in* L. Casson, The Ancient Mariners. From the dim beginnings of sea-conquest to the great maritime empires of Antiquity, London, 1959, pp. 4-9.

1092 R.H. BRUNSWIG, Indus-Persian Gulf Contact, *in* Radiocarbon Dating and the Indus Civilization: Calibration and Chronology, *in* East and West 25/1-2, 1975, pp. 117-120.

1093 G.F. HOURANI, Arab Seafaring in the Indian Ocean in Ancient and Early Medieval Times, [= Reprint of Volume 13, Princeton Oriental Studies, 1951], New York, 1975, xi + 131 p., 8 Pl., VII maps.

1094 P.B. CORNWALL, On the Location of Dilmun, [= Reprint of BASOR 103, 1946, pp. 3-11], *in* Ancient Cities of the Indus (G.L. Possehl, ed.), New Delhi, 1979, pp. 164-167.

1095 C.J. GADD, Seals of Ancient Indian Style Found at Ur, *in* Ancient Cities of the Indus (G.L. Possehl, ed.), [= Reprint from the Proceedings of the British Academy 18, 1932, pp. 3-22], New Delhi, 1979, pp. 115-122, Pl. VI-VIII.

1096 S.N. KRAMER, The Indus Civilization and Dilmun: The Sumerian Paradise Land, *in* Ancient Cities of the Indus (G.L. Possehl, ed.), New Delhi, 1979, pp. 168-173.

1097 P. CALMEYER, Zur Genese altiranischer Motive VIII. Die "statistische Landcharte des Perserreiches" I, *in* Archäologische Mitteilungen aus Iran, Neue Folge, Bd. 15, Berlin, 1982, pp. 105-187, Abb. 1-10, Tab. 16-24.

1098 W.F. LEEMANS, Foreign trade in the Old Babylonian period as revealed by texts from southern Mesopotamia [= Studia et Documenta ad Iura Orientis Antiqui Pertinentia 6], Reprint, 1982, vii + 196 p., 2 maps.

1099 H. MÜLLER-KARPE, Zur Seefahrt im 3. und 2. Jahrtausend vor Chr., *in* Zur geschichtlichen Bedeutung der frühen Seefahrt (H. Müller-Karpe, ed.), [= Kommission für Allgemeine und Vergleichende Archäologie des Deutschen Archäologischen Instituts, Bonn], München, 1982, pp. 1-20, 10 Abb.

1100 P. CALMEYER, Zur Genese altiranischer Motive VIII. Die "statistische Landcharte des Perserreiches" II, *in* Archäologische Mitteilungen aus Iran, Neue Folge, Bd. 16, Berlin, 1983, pp. 141-222, Abb. 10a-14.

1101 E.C.L. DURING CASPERS, Review of Shereen Ratnagar: Encounters. The Westerly Trade of the Harappan Civilization, *in* Bibliotheca Orientalis XL/3-4, 1983, pp. 494-502.

1102 S. CLEUZIOU, Oman peninsula and its relations eastwards during Third Millennium, *in* Frontiers of the Indus Civilization (B.B. Lal & S.P. Gupta, eds.) [= Sir Mortimer Wheeler Commemoration Volume], New Delhi, 1984, pp. 371-394, 29 fig.

1103 T. MAEDA, "King of the Four Regions" in the Dynasty of Akkade, *in* Orient XX, 1984, pp. 67-82.

1104 M. SPEECE, The Role of Eastern Arabia in the Arabian Gulf Trade of the Third and Second Millennia, *in* Pre-Islamic Arabia. Studies in the History of Arabia II [= Proceedings of the Second International Symposium on Studies in the History of Arabia 1399/1979], Riyadh, 1984, pp. 167-176.

1105 G. BIBBY, "The Land of Dilmun is holy...", *in* Dilmun 12, 1984-'85, pp. 3-4.

1106 C.C. LAMBERG-KARLOVSKY, Death in Dilmun, *in* Dilmun 12, 1984-'85, pp. 15-24.

1107 G. WEISGERBER, Dilmun — a trading entrepot: evidence from historical and archaeological sources, *in* Dilmun 12, 1984-'85, pp. 5-10.

1108 T. BERTHOUD, La métallurgie du cuivre aux IVe et IIIe millénaires, *in* Le Proche-Orient ancien. Le Grand Atlas de l'Archéologie [Encyclopaedia Universalis], Paris, 1985, pp. 188-189, 6 fig.

1109 S.C. BROWN, Mesopotamia and South Asia (Indus Valley): Reciprocal Effects in the Late 3rd and Early 2nd Millennia B.C., *in* Bulletin 9 [= The Society for Mesopotamian Studies], May 1985, pp. 15-24.

1110 S. CLEUZIOU, Zwischen Sumer und Meluchcha: Magan, *in* Das Altertum 31/3, 1985, pp. 141-150, 7 fig.

1111 E.C.L. DURING CASPERS, A Note on Two Stamp Seals from the Arabian Gulf Area, *in* Annali dell'Istituto Universitario Orientale 45/2, Napoli, 1985, pp. 313-315, 1 Pl.

1112 C.C. LAMBERG-KARLOVSKY, The Longue Durée of the Ancient Near East, *in* De l'Indus aux Balkans, Recueil à la Mémoire de Jean Deshayes (J.-L. Huot, M. Yon & Y. Calvet, eds.), Paris, 1985, pp. 55-72.

1113 P.R.S. MOOREY, The Gulf and the route to the Indus Valley: Dilmun, Magan und Meluhha, *in* Materials and Manufacture in Ancient Mesopotamia. The Evidence of Archaeology and Art. Metals and Metal-work, glazed materials and glass [= BAR (British Archaeological Reports), International Series 237], Oxford, 1985, pp. XVII-XXII.

1114 J.D. MUHLY, Sources of Tin and the Beginnings of Bronze Metallurgy, *in* American Journal of Archaeology 89/2, 1985, pp. 275-291, 5 fig.

1115 P. AMIET, Susa and the Dilmun Culture, *in* Bahrain through the ages, the Archaeology (Shaikha Haya Ali al-Khalifa & M. Rice, eds.), London, 1986, pp. 262-268, fig. 85-95.

1116 G. BIBBY, "The Land of Dilmun is holy...", *in* Bahrain through the ages, the Archaeology (Shaikha Haya Ali al-Khalifa & M. Rice, eds.), London, 1986, pp. 192-194.

1117 R.M. BOEHMER, Einflüsse der Golfglyptik auf die anatolische Stempel-glyptik zur Zeit der assyrischen Handelsniederlassungen, *in* Baghdader Mitteilungen 17, 1986, pp. 293-298, 1 Abb., Taf. 42-44.

1118 S. CLEUZIOU, Dilmun and Makkan during the third and early second mil-lennia B.C., *in* Bahrain through the ages, the Archaeology (Shaikha Haya Ali al-Khalifa & M. Rice, eds.), London, 1986, pp. 143-155.

1119 A.H. DANI, Bahrain and the Indus civilisation, *in* Bahrain through the ages, the Archaeology (Shaikha Haya Ali al-Khalifa & M. Rice, eds.), London, 1986, pp. 383-388.

1120 E.C.L. DURING CASPERS, Animal design and Gulf chronology, *in* Bahrain through the ages, the Archaeology (Shaikha Haya Ali al-Khalifa & M. Rice, eds.), London, 1986, pp. 286-304, fig. 119-124.

1121 E.C.L. DURING CASPERS, Of corals and ailments in the Ancient Near East, *in* Proceedings of the Seminar for Arabian Studies 16 [= Proceedings of the 19th Seminar for Arabian Studies 1985], 1986, pp. 25-31.

1122 T. HOWARD-CARTER, Eyestones and Pearls, *in* Bahrain through the ages, the Archaeology (Shaikha Haya Ali al-Khalifa & M. Rice, eds.), London, 1986, pp. 305-310, fig. 125-129.

1123 J.P. JOSHI, India and Bahrain: A survey of culture interaction during the third and second millennia, *in* Bahrain through the ages, the Archaeology (Shaikha Haya Ali al-Khalifa & M. Rice, eds.), London, 1986, pp. 72-75.

1124 P. KJÆRUM, The Dilmun seals as evidence of long distance relations in the early second millennium B.C., *in* Bahrain through the ages, the Archaeo-logy (Shaikha Haya Ali al-Khalifa & M. Rice, eds.), London, 1986, pp. 269-277, fig. 96-105.

1125 P.L. KOHL, The lands of Dilmun: changing cultural and economic rela-tions during the third to early second millennia B.C., *in* Bahrain through the ages, the Archaeology (Shaikha Haya Ali al-Khalifa & M. Rice, eds.), London, 1986, pp. 367-375.

1126 C.C. LAMBERG-KARLOVSKY, Death in Dilmun, *in* Bahrain through the ages, the Archaeology (Shaikha Haya Ali al-Khalifa & M. Rice, eds.), London, 1986, pp. 156-165.

1127 C.C. LAMBERG-KARLOVSKY, Third Millennium Structure and Process: From the Euphrates to the Indus and the Oxus to the Indian Ocean, *in* Oriens Antiquus XXV/3-4, 1986, pp. 189-219, 5 fig.

1128 T.C. MITCHELL, Indus and Gulf type seals from Ur, *in* Bahrain through the ages, the Archaeology (Shaikha Haya Ali al-Khalifa & M. Rice, eds.), London, 1986, pp. 278-285, fig. 106-118, 1 Tab.

1129 K. NASHEF, The Deities of Dilmun, *in* Bahrain through the ages, the Archaeology (Shaikha Haya Ali al-Khalifa & M. Rice, eds.), London, 1986, pp. 340-366.

1130 H.J. NISSEN, The occurence of Dilmun in the oldest texts of Mesopotamia, *in* Bahrain through the ages, the Archaeology (Shaikha Haya Ali al-Khalifa & M. Rice, eds.), London, 1986, pp. 335-339.

1131 D.T. POTTS, Dilmun's further relations: the Syro-Anatolian evidence from the third and second millennia B.C., *in* Bahrain through the ages, the Archaeology (Shaikha Haya Ali al-Khalifa & M. Rice, eds.), London, 1986, pp. 389-398.

1132 D.T. POTTS, The Booty of Magan, *in* Oriens Antiquus XXV/3-4, 1986, pp. 271-285, Pl. XXII-XXXI.

1133 D.T. POTTS, Nippur and Dilmun in the 14th Century B.C., *in* Proceedings of the Seminar for Arabian Studies 16 [= Proceedings of the 19th Seminar for Arabian Studies 1985], 1986, pp. 169-174.

1134 S.R. RAO, Trade and cultural contacts between Bahrain and India in the third and second millennia B.C., *in* Bahrain through the ages, the Archaeology (Shaikha Haya Ali al-Khalifa & M. Rice, eds.), London, 1986, pp. 376-382, fig. 138-143.

1135 J. READE, Commerce or Conquest: variations in the Mesopotamia-Dilmun relationship, *in* Bahrain through the ages, the Archaeology (Shaikha Haya Ali al-Khalifa & M. Rice, eds.), London, 1986, pp. 325-334, fig. 136-137.

1136 M. RICE, "The island on the edge of the world", *in* Bahrain through the ages, the Archaeology (Shaikha Haya Ali al-Khalifa & M. Rice, eds.), London, 1986, pp. 116-124.

1137 G. WEISGERBER, Dilmun — A trading entrepôt: evidence from historical and archaeological sources, *in* Bahrain through the ages, the Archaeology (Shaikha Haya Ali al-Khalifa & M. Rice, eds.), London, 1986, pp. 135-142.

1138 C. Zaccagnini, The Dilmun Standard and its relationship with Indus and Near Eastern Weight Systems, *in* Iraq 48, 1986, pp. 19-23.

1139 J. Zarins, MAR-TU and the land of Dilmun, *in* Bahrain through the ages, the Archaeology (Shaikha Haya Ali al-Khalifa & M. Rice, eds.), London, 1986, pp. 233-250, fig. 68.

1140 E.A. Braun-Holzinger, Nochmals zu Naramsins "Beute von Magan", *in* Oriens Antiquus 26/3-4, 1987, pp. 285-290.

1141 E.C.L. During Caspers, A Copper-Bronze Animal in Harappan Style from Bahrain: Evidence of Mercantile Interaction, *in* Journal of the Economic and Social History of the Orient XXX/1, 1987, pp. 30-46, 4 fig.

1142 E.C.L. During Caspers, In the footsteps of Gilgamesh: in search of the "Prickly Rose", *in* Persica XII, 1987, pp. 57-95, 4 Pl.

1143 W. Heimpel, Das Untere Meer, *in* Zeitschrift für Assyriologie und Vorderasiatische Archäologie 77/1, 1987, pp. 22-91, 4 Abb., 2 Tab.

1144 M. Tosi, Die Indus-Zivilisation jenseits des indischen Subkontinents, *in* Vergessene Städte am Indus. Frühe Kulturen in Pakistan vom 8.–2. Jahrtausend v. Chr., Mainz am Rhein, 1987, pp. 119-136, Abb. 93-108.

1145 W. Heimpel, Magan, *in* Reallexikon der Assyriologie und Vorderasiatischen Archäologie 7/3-4, 1988, pp. 195-199.

1146 C.C. Lamberg-Karlovsky, The "Intercultural Style" Carved Vessels, *in* Iranica Antiqua XXIII, 1988, pp. 45-95, 4 fig., X Pl.

1147 P. Michalowski, Magan and Meluhha Once Again, *in* Journal of Cuneiform Studies 40/2, 1988, pp. 156-164.

1148 J.E. Dayton, The Problem of Magan and Meluhha, Appendix II to J.E. Dayton, The Faience of the Indus Civilization, *in* South Asian Archaeology 1985 (K. Frifelt & P. Sørensen, eds.) [= Scandinavian Institute of Asian Studies Occasional Papers 4 — Papers from the Eighth International Conference of South Asian Archaeologists in Western Europe, Moesgaard, 1985], London & Riverdale, 1989, p. 225.

1149 J.J. Glassner, Mesopotamian textual evidence on Magan/Makan in the late 3rd millennium B.C., *in* Oman Studies, Papers on the archaeology and history of Oman [= Serie Orientale Roma 63 (P.M. Costa & M. Tosi, eds.)], Roma, 1989, pp. 181-191, 2 Pl.

1150 F. Højlund, Dilmun and the Sealand, *in* Northern Akkad Project Reports 2 (L. De Meyer & H. Gasche, eds.), Gent, 1989, pp. 9-14, 7 fig.

1151 F. Højlund, Some New Evidence of Harappan Influence in the Arabian Gulf, *in* South Asian Archaeology 1985 (K. Frifelt & P. Sørensen, eds.) [= Scandinavian Institute of Asian Studies Occasional Papers 4 — Papers from the Eighth International Conference of South Asian Archaeologists in Western Europe, Moesgaard, 1985], London & Riverdale, 1989, pp. 49-53, 7 fig.

1152 F. Højlund, Dilmun und Bahrain. Zur Herausbildung des ersten arabischen Staates, *in* Das Altertum 35/2, 1989, pp. 113-118, 4 fig.

1153 T.F. Potts, Foreign Stone Vessels of the Late Third Millennium B.C. from Southern Mesopotamia: Their Origins and Mechanism of Exchange, *in* Iraq LI, 1989, pp. 123-164, 13 fig., 2 Tab.

1154 S. Zakri, Oman et la Mer. Les plus anciens marins, *in* Archéologia 248, juillet-âout 1989, pp. 46-53, 9 fig.

1155 D.K. Chakrabarti, The Persian Gulf, *in* The External Trade of the Indus Civilization, New Delhi, 1990, pp. 13-20.

1156 E.C.L. During Caspers, "...and Multi-coloured Birds of Meluhha", *in* Proceedings of the Seminar for Arabian Studies 20 [= Proceedings of the 23rd Seminar for Arabian Studies, held at London on 18th–20th July 1989], 1990, pp. 9-16, 9 Pl.

1157 M. Rice, Eastwards from Egypt, *in* Egypt's Making. The Origins of Ancient Egypt, 5000–2000 BC, London & New York, 1990, pp. 242-263, fig. 104-111.

1158 E.C.L. During Caspers, The Indus Valley "Unicorn". A Near Eastern Connection?, *in* Journal of the Economic and Social History of the Orient XXXIV/3, 1991, pp. 312-350.

1159 P. Kjærum, The Ships of Dilmun, *in* Folk 33, 1991, pp. 137-147.

1160 G. Weisgerber, Die Suche nach dem altsumerischen Kupferland Makan, *in* Das Altertum 37/2, 1991, pp. 76-90, 15 fig.

1161 H. Crawford, Patterns of trade in Mesopotamia 3500–2500 BC, *in* Dilmun 15, 1991-'92, pp. 17-21.

1162 J. Aruz, Persian Gulf Stamp Seal with two Caprids, *in* The Royal City of Susa. Ancient Near Eastern Treasures in the Louvre [The Metropolitan Museum of Art, New York], New York, 1992, p. 119, fig. 78.

1163 J. Aruz, Cylinder Seal from the Persian Gulf, *in* The Royal City of Susa. Ancient Near Eastern Treasures in the Louvre [The Metropolitan Museum of Art, New York], New York, 1992, p. 119, fig. 79.

1164 S. Cleuziou, The Oman Peninsula and the Indus Civilization: A reassessment, *in* Man and Environment 17/2, 1992, pp. 93-103.

1165 E.C.L. During Caspers, Intercultural/Mercantile Contacts between the Arabian Gulf and South Asia at the Close of the Third Millennium B.C., *in* Proceedings of the Seminar for Arabian Studies 22 [= Proceedings of the 25th Seminar for Arabian Studies, held at Cambridge on 23rd–25th July 1991], 1992, pp. 3-28, 10 Pl.

1166 S. Kay, Most Ancient of Routes, *in* Seafarers of the Gulf, Dubai, 1992, pp. 4-11, 8 fig.

1167 G. WEISGERBER, Slag heap search for Magan, *in* PDO News [= Petroleum Development Oman News], Muscat, 1992-2, pp. 16-23, 24 fig.

1168 J. EIDEM & F. HØJLUND, Trade or diplomacy? Assyria and Dilmun in the Eighteenth Century BC, *in* World Archaeology 24/3 [= Ancient Trade: New Perspectives (J. Oates, ed.)], 1993, pp. 441-448, 1 fig., 2 Pl.

1169 D.T. POTTS, Rethinking some aspects of trade in the Arabian Gulf, *in* World Archaeology 24/3 [= Ancient Trade: New Perspectives (J. Oates, ed.)], 1993, pp. 423-440, 7 fig., 3 Pl., 2 Tab.

1170 T.F. POTTS, Patterns of trade in third-millennium BC Mesopotamia and Iran, *in* World Archaeology 24/3 [= Ancient Trade: New Perspectives (J. Oates, ed.)], 1993, pp. 379-402, 5 fig.

1171 J. ARUZ, Cachet du Golfe Persique avec deux caprins, *in* La cité royale de Suse: Trésors du Proche-Orient ancien au Louvre [= Edition française révisée par A. Caubet], Paris, 1994, pp. 119-120, ill.

1172 J. ARUZ, Sceau-cylindre du Golfe Persique à la divinité assise, *in* La cité royale de Suse: Trésors du Proche-Orient ancien au Louvre [= Edition française révisée par A. Caubet], Paris, 1994, p. 120, ill.

1173 E.C.L. DURING CASPERS, Non-Indus Glyptics in a Harappan Context, *in* Iranica Antiqua XXIX [= Festschrift K. Schippmann I], 1994, pp. 83-106, 4 Pl.

1174 P.R.S. MOOREY, Building with wood. II. Sources outside Mesopotamia. c. In the Gulf and regions beyond to the Indus Valley, *in* P.R.S. Moorey, Ancient Mesopotamian Materials and Industries. The Archaeological Evidence, Oxford, 1994, pp. 352-353.

1175 S. ZAKRI, Sultanat d'Oman: Bât et les routes de commerce de l'âge du Bronze, *in* Archéologia 306, 1994, pp. 60-66.

1176 H. CRAWFORD & K. al-SINDI, A seal in the collections of the National Museum, Bahrain, *in* Arabian archaeology and epigraphy 6/1, 1995, pp. 1-4, 2 fig.

1177 U. FRANKE-VOGT, Der Golfhandel im späten 3. und frühen 2. Jt. v. Chr., *in* Zwischen Euphrat und Indus. Aktuelle Forschungsprobleme in der Vorderasiatischen Archäologie (K. Bartl, R. Bernbeck & M. Heinz, eds.), Hildesheim, 1995, pp. 114-133, Abb.

1178 A. HAMOTO, Dilmun, *in* Der Affe in der altorientalischen Kunst [= Forschungen zur Anthropologie und Religionsgeschichte 28], Münster, 1995, pp. 23-26, 153-155, Abb. 21-34.

1179 D.T. POTTS, Watercraft of the Lower Sea, *in* Beiträge zur Kulturgeschichte Vorderasiens. Festschrift für Rainer Michael Boehmer (U. Finkbeiner, R. Dittmann & H. Hauptmann, Hrsg.), Mainz, 1995, pp. 559-571, 14 fig., Pl. 42g.

1180 J. READE, Magan and Meluhhan Merchants at Ur, *in* Beiträge zur Kulturgeschichte Vorderasiens. Festschrift für Rainer Michael Boehmer (U. Finkbeiner, R. Dittmann & H. Hauptmann, Hrsg.), Mainz, 1995, pp. 597-600, Pl. 43-45.

1181 F.H. VAN DIJK, Scheepvaart in de Perzische Golf: maritieme contacten in het derde millennium voor Christus, *in* Phoenix 41/2, 1995, pp. 64-71, 4 fig.

LATE 2ND MILLENNIUM B.C. — 7TH CENTURY A.D.

General studies

1182 I. KAWAR, The Arabs in the Peace Treaty of A.D. 561, *in* Arabica 3, 1956, pp. 181-213.

1183 F. ALTHEIM & R. STIEHL, Die Araber zwischen Alexander und Mohammed, *in* Das Altertum 8/2, 1962, pp. 102-113, 1 fig.

1184 H. SCHIWEK, Der Persische Golf als Schiffahrts- und Seehandelsroute in Achämenidischer Zeit und in der Zeit Alexanders des Grossen, *in* Bonner Jahrbücher 162, Bonn, 1962, pp. 4-97.

1185 J. TEIXIDOR, Monnaies d'Arabie du Nord trouvées à Suse, *in* Bulletin d'épigraphie sémitique 1970, n°. 54, *in* Syria XLVII, 1970, pp. 365-366, fig. 1.

1186 G. LE RIDER, Les monnaies de bronze de Séleucie du Tigre à Suse sous les Séleucides et les Parthes et la navigation dans le Golfe Persique, *in* Sociétés et Compagnies de Commerce en Orient et dans l'Océan Indien (M. Mollat, ed.), 1971, pp. 121-127, 1 fig.

1187 H. SEYRIG, Une question de numismatique gréco-arabe, *in* Bulletin d'Etudes Orientales 25, 1972, pp. 1-3.

1188 M.G. RASCHKE, New Studies in Roman Commerce with the East, *in* Aufstieg und Niedergang der Römischen Welt II-9,2 (H. Temporini & W. Haase, eds.), Berlin & New York, 1978, pp. 605-1363, 6 maps, II Pl.

1189 E.C.L. DURING CASPERS, Westward Contacts with Historical India: A Trio of Figurines, *in* Proceedings of the Seminar for Arabian Studies 9 [= Proceedings of the 12th Seminar for Arabian Studies 1978], 1979, pp. 10-30, VII Pl.

1190 R. ZADOK, Arabians in Mesopotamia during the Late-Assyrian, Chaldean, Achaemenian and Hellenistic Periods, *in* Zeitschrift der Deutschen Morgenländischen Gesellschaft 131, 1981, pp. 42-84, 3 Tab.

1191 M. O'DWYER SHEA, The small cuboid incense-burner of the ancient Near East, *in* Levant XV, 1983, pp. 76-109.

1192 W.C. BRICE, The Classical Trade-Routes of Arabia, from the Evidence of Ptolemy, Strabo and Pliny, *in* Pre-Islamic Arabia. Studies in the History of Arabia II [= Proceedings of the Second International Symposium on Studies in the History of Arabia 1399/1979], Riyadh, 1984, pp. 177-181, maps 9-10.

1193 L. CASSON, Patterns of Seaborne Trade in the First Century A.D., *in* Bulletin of the American Society of Papyrologists 21, 1984, pp. 39-47.

1194 W.W. MÜLLER, Survey of the History of the Arabian Peninsula from the First Century A.D. to the Rise of Islam, *in* Pre-Islamic Arabia. Studies in the History of Arabia II [= Proceedings of the Second International Symposium on Studies in the History of Arabia 1399/1979], Riyadh, 1984, pp. 125-131.

1195 V.F. PIACENTINI, La presa di potere sasanide sul Golfo Persico fra leggenda e realtà, *in* Clio 20/2, 1984, pp. 173-211, 1 carte.

1196 V.F. PIACENTINI, Haftanboht e Mihrak: La discesa sasanide al Golfo Persico fra leggenda e realtà, *in* Studi in onore di Francesco Gabrieli nel suo ottantesimo compleanno (R. Traini, ed.), Roma, 1984, pp. 323-339, 1 carte.

1197 P. HÖGEMANN, Alexander der Grosse und Arabien, *in* Zetemata, Monographien zur klassischen Altertumswissenschaft 82, München, 1985, x + 236 p.

1198 V.F. PIACENTINI, Ardashir i Papakan and the wars against the Arabs: working Hypothesis on the Sasanian Hold of the Gulf, *in* Proceedings of the Seminar for Arabian Studies 15 [= Proceedings of the 18th Seminar for Arabian Studies 1984], 1985, pp. 57-77, 2 fig.

1199 A. ANANI & K. WHITTINGHAM, The Early History of the Gulf Arabs, London & New York, 1986, vi + 170 p. (espec. pp. 1-73), 3 maps.

1200 L. CASSON, P. Vindob. G 40822 and the shipping of goods from India, *in* Bulletin of the American Society of Papyrologists 23/3-4, 1986, pp. 73-79.

1201 N. GROOM, Eastern Arabia in Ptolemy's map, *in* Proceedings of the Seminar for Arabian Studies 16 [= Proceedings of the 19th Seminar for Arabian Studies 1985], 1986, pp. 65-75, 3 fig.

1202 H. SEYRIG, Une question de numismatique gréco-arabe, *in* Scripta numismatica, 1986, pp. 7-10.

1203 R. BOUCHARLAT & J.-F. SALLES, L'Arabie Orientale: d'un bilan à un autre, *in* Mesopotamia XXII, 1987, pp. 277-309, fig. A-I.

1204 M.G. MORONY, The Arabisation of the Gulf, *in* The Arab Gulf and the Arab World (B.R. Pridham, ed.), London, New York & Sydney, 1987, pp. 3-28.

1205 D.T. POTTS, Palmyra, Charax og den Persiske Golf, *in* Dagligliv blandt guder og mennesker (B. Alster & P.J. Frandsen, eds.), Den naere Orient i oldtiden, 1987, pp. 195-201, 2 fig.

1206 J.-F. SALLES, The Arab-Persian Gulf under the Seleucids, *in* Hellenism in the East. The Interaction of Greek and non-Greek civilizations from Syria to Central Asia after Alexander (A. Kuhrt & S. Sherwin-White, eds.), London, 1987, pp. 75-109 & 163-184, 3 fig.

1207 J. TEIXIDOR, Parthian Officials in Lower Mesopotamia, *in* Mesopotamia XXII, 1987, pp. 187-193.

1208 R. BOUCHARLAT, Entre la Méditerranée et l'Inde. Etablissements du Golfe Persique à l'époque gréco-romaine, *in* Revue Archéologique XXI [= Bulletin de la Société Française d'Archéologie Classique], 1987-'88, pp. 214-220, 3 fig.

1209 E.C.L. DURING CASPERS, Contacts between India and the West during early historical times, *in* Indian Museum Bulletin XXI (1986), 1988, pp. 22-33, VIII Pl.

1210 D.T. POTTS, Arabia and the Kingdom of Characene, *in* Araby the Blest. Studies in Arabian Archaeology (D.T. Potts, ed.), Margaret Golding in Memoriam [= Carsten Niebuhr Institute Publications 7], Copenhagen, 1988, pp. 136-167, 2 fig.

1211 R. BOUCHARLAT, Cairns et pseudo-cairns du Fars. L'utilisation des tombes de surface au 1er millénaire de notre ère, *in* Archaeologia Iranica et Orientalis, Miscellanea in honorem Louis Vanden Berghe (L. De Meyer & E. Haerinck, eds.), Gent, 1989, pp. 675-712, 3 fig., V Pl.

1212 G.W. BOWERSOCK, La Mésène (Maisan) Antonine, *in* L'Arabie préislamique et son environnement historique et culturel [= Actes du Colloque de Strasbourg, 24–27 juin 1987 (T. Fahd, ed.)], Leiden, 1989, pp. 159-168.

1213 G. LE RIDER, Le Golfe Persique à l'époque séleucide: exploration archéologique et trouvailles monétaires, *in* Revue numismatique XXXI, 1989, pp. 248-252, 1 map.

1214 A. LIVINGSTONE, Arabians in Babylonia — Babylonians in Arabia. Some reflections à propos new and old evidence, *in* L'Arabie préislamique et son environnement historique et culturel [= Actes du Colloque de Strasbourg, 24–27 juin 1987 (T. Fahd, ed.)], Leiden, 1989, pp. 97-105, 2 fig.

1215 P. LOMBARD, Ages du Fer sans fer: le cas de la péninsule d'Oman au 1er millénaire avant J.C., *in* L'Arabie préislamique et son environnement historique et culturel [= Actes du Colloque de Strasbourg, 24–27 juin 1987 (T. Fahd, ed.)], Leiden, 1989, pp. 25-37, 1 fig.

1216 H.I. MACADAM, Strabo, Pliny the Elder and Ptolemy of Alexandria: Three Views of Ancient Arabia and its People, *in* L'Arabie préislamique et son environnement historique et culturel [= Actes du Colloque de Strasbourg, 24–27 juin 1987 (T. Fahd, ed.)], Leiden, 1989, pp. 289-320, fig.

1217 J.-P. REY-COQUAIS, L'Arabie dans les routes de commerce entre le monde méditerranéen et les côtes indiennes, *in* L'Arabie préislamique et son environnement historique et culturel [= Actes du Colloque de Strasbourg, 24–27 juin 1987 (T. Fahd, ed.)], Leiden, 1989, pp. 225-239.

1218 J.-F. SALLES, Les échanges commerciaux et culturels dans le Golfe arabo-persique au 1er millénaire avant J.C.: Reflexions sur Makkan et Meluhha, *in* L'Arabie préislamique et son environnement historique et culturel [= Actes du Colloque de Strasbourg, 24–27 juin 1987 (T. Fahd, ed.)], Leiden, 1989, pp. 67-96, 1 fig.

1219 O. CALLOT, Les monnaies dites "arabes" dans le nord du Golfe arabo-persique à la fin du IIIe siècle avant notre ère, *in* Failaka. Fouilles françaises 1986-1988 (Y. Calvet & J. Gachet, eds.) [= Travaux de la Maison de l'Orient 18], Lyon, 1990, pp. 221-240, 13 fig.

1220 D.F. GRAF, Arabia during Achaemenid times, *in* Achaemenid History IV. Centre and Periphery, Proceedings of the Groningen 1986 Achaemenid History Workshop (H. Sancisi-Weerdenburg & A. Kuhrt, eds.), Leiden, 1990, pp. 131-148, 1 fig.

1221 L. HANNESTAD, Change and Conservatism. Hellenistic Pottery in Mesopotamia and Iran, *in* Akten des XIII. Internationalen Kongresses für Klassische Archäologie, Berlin 1988, Mainz am Rhein, 1990, pp. 179-186, 4 fig.

1222 D.T. POTTS, The Arabian Gulf in Antiquity II. Alexander the Great to the Coming of Islam, Oxford, 1990, xxi +369 p., 1 map, 25 fig., 2 Tab., XII Pl.

1223 J.-F. SALLES, Les Achéménides dans le Golfe Arabo-Persique, *in* Achaemenid History IV. Centre and Periphery, Proceedings of the Groningen 1986 Achaemenid History Workshop (H. Sancisi-Weerdenburg & A. Kuhrt, eds.), Leiden, 1990, pp. 111-130, 1 fig.

1224 C. ARNOLD-BIUCCHI, Arabian Alexanders, *in* Mnemata: Papers in Memory of Nancy M. Waggoner [= The American Numismatic Society], 1991, pp. 99-115, 1 fig., Pl. 18-21.

1225 E. DABROVA, Die Politik der Arsakiden auf dem gebiet des Südlichen Mesopotamiens und im Becken des Persischen Meerbusens in der zweiten Hälfte des 1. Jahrhunderts n. Chr., *in* Mesopotamia XXVI, 1991, pp. 141-153.

1226 B.E. DENTON, The Late Second Millennium B.C. in the Arab/Iranian Gulf, Bryn Mawr College. Dr. of Philosophy [= UMI 9212994], 1991, XIV + 324 p., 70 fig., 5 maps.

1227 G. GROPP, Christian Maritime Trade of Sasanian Age in the Persian Gulf, *in* Golf–Archäologie. Mesopotamien, Iran, Kuwait, Bahrain, Vereinigte Arabische Emirate und Oman (K. Schippmann, A. Herling & J.-F. Salles, eds.) [= Internationale Archäologie 6, Buch am Erlbach], Göttingen & Lyon, 1991, pp. 83-88, 1 map.

1228 L. HANNESTAD, The Greeks in the region of the Arabian Gulf, *in* O ELLHNISMOS ETHN ANATOLH (Hellenism in the East), International

Meeting of History and Archaeology, Delphi 6-9 Nov. 1986, European Cultural Centre of Delphi, Athens, 1991, pp. 41-56.

1229 S. KROLL, Zu den Beziehungen eisenzeitlicher bemalter Keramikkomplexe in Oman und Iran, *in* Golf–Archäologie. Mesopotamien, Iran, Kuwait, Bahrain, Vereinigte Arabische Emirate und Oman (K. Schippmann, A. Herling & J.-F. Salles, eds.) [= Internationale Archäologie 6, Buch am Erlbach], Göttingen & Lyon, 1991, pp. 315-320, 1 fig.

1230 D.T. POTTS, The Pre-Islamic Coinage of Eastern Arabia [= Carsten Niebuhr Institute Publications 14], Copenhagen, 1991, 119 p., 529 fig., Fig. A-B, 4 Tab.

1231 C.J. HOWGEGO & D.T. POTTS, Greek and Roman coins from Eastern Arabia, *in* Arabian archaeology and epigraphy 3/3, 1992, pp. 183-189, 18 fig.

1232 S. KAY, Greeks and Romans, *in* Seafarers of the Gulf, Dubai, 1992, pp. 12-17, 6 fig.

1233 H.M. al-NABOODAH, The Commercial Activity of Bahrain and Oman in the Early Middle Ages, *in* Proceedings of the Seminar for Arabian Studies 22 [= Proceedings of the 25th Seminar for Arabian Studies, held at Cambridge on 23rd–25th July 1991], 1992, pp. 81-96, 2 fig.

1234 Y. OKADA, Ain Sha'ia and the Early Gulf Churches: An Architectural Analogy, *in* al-Rafidan XIII, 1992, pp. 87-93, 1 fig.

1235 J.-F. SALLES, Review of "D.T. Potts: The Arabian Gulf in Antiquity, Vol. II. From Alexander the Great to the Coming of Islam, Oxford, 1990", *in* Topoi 2, 1992, pp. 201-235, 1 map.

1236 J.-F. SALLES, Découvertes du Golfe Arabo-Persique aux époques grecque et romaine, *in* L'Océan et les mers lointaines dans l'antiquité. [= Actes du colloque de la Société des Professeurs d'Histoire Ancienne de l'Université, Nantes-Angers 24-26 mai 1991], Revue des Etudes Anciennes 94, 1-2, 1992, pp. 79-97, 1 map.

1237 R. BOUCHARLAT & M. MOUTON, Importations occidentales et influence de l'hellénisme dans la péninsule d'Oman, *in* Arabia Antiqua. Hellenistic Centres around Arabia [= Serie Orientale Roma 70, II (A. Invernizzi & J.-F. Salles, eds.)], Roma, 1993, pp. 275-289, 6 fig.

1238 E.C.L. DURING CASPERS, Review of D.T. Potts "Araby the Blest. Studies in Arabian Archaeology", Copenhagen, *in* Bibliotheca Orientalis L/5-6, 1993, pp. 735-739.

1239 U. FINKBEINER, Vergleichende Stratigraphie und Chronologie, *in* Materialien zur Archäologie der Seleukiden- und Partherzeit im südlichen Babylonien und im Golfgebiet (U. Finkbeiner, ed.) [= Ergebnisse der

Symposien 1987 und 1989 in Blaubeuren (Deutsches Archäologisches Institut, Abteilung Baghdad)], Tübingen, 1993, pp. 281-288, 1 Abb., 2 Tab.

1240 M. Maraqten, Wine drinking and wine prohibition in Arabia before Islam, *in* Proceedings of the Seminar for Arabian Studies 23 [= Proceedings of the 26th Seminar for Arabian Studies, held at Manchester 1992], 1993, pp. 95-115.

1241 J.-F. Salles, The Periplus of the Erythraean Sea and the Arab-Persian Gulf, *in* Topoi 3/2, 1993, pp. 493-524, 2 maps.

1242 J. Teixidor, Historiographical Sources and Absolute Chronology, *in* Materialien zur Archäologie der Seleukiden- und Partherzeit im südlichen Babylonien und im Golfgebiet (U. Finkbeiner, ed.) [= Ergebnisse der Symposien 1987 und 1989 in Blaubeuren (Deutsches Archäologisches Institut, Abteilung Baghdad)], Tübingen, 1993, pp. 289-294.

1243 N. Groom, Oman and the Emirates in Ptolemy's map, *in* Arabian archaeology and epigraphy 5/3, 1994, pp. 198-214, 2 maps.

1244 E. Haerinck, Un service à boire décoré — A propos d'iconographie arabique préislamique, *in* Mesopotamian History and Environment. Occasional Publications III. Cinquante-deux reflexions sur le Proche-Orient Ancien offertes en hommage à Leon De Meyer (H. Gasche, M. Tanret, C. Janssen & A. Degraeve, eds.), Leuven, 1994, pp. 401-426, 4 fig., VIII Pl.

1245 D.T. Potts, Supplement to the Pre-Islamic Coinage of Eastern Arabia [= Carsten Niebuhr Institute Publications 16], Copenhagen, 1994, 88 p., 426 ill., maps, 5 Tab.

1246 J.-F. Salles, Le Golfe arabo-persique entre Séleucides et Maurya, *in* Topoi 4/2, 1994, pp. 597-610.

1247 J.-F. Salles, Fines Indiae, Ardh el-Hind. Recherches sur le devenir de la mer Erythrée, *in* The Roman and Byzantine Army in the East. Proceedings of a colloqium held at the Jagiellonian University, Krakow in September 1992 (E. Dabrowa, ed.), Krakow, 1994, pp. 165-187.

1248 M. Tardieu, L'Arabie du Nord-Est d'après les documents manichéens, *in* Studia Iranica 23/1, 1994, pp. 59-75.

1249 N. Groom, The Periplus, Pliny and Arabia, *in* Arabian archaeology and epigraphy 6/3, 1995, pp. 180-195.

1250 J.-F. Salles, The Periplus of the Eythraean Sea and the Arab-Persian Gulf, *in* Athens, Aden, Arikamedu. Essays on the interrelations between India, Arabia and the Eastern Mediterranean (M.-F. Boussac & J.-F. Salles, eds.) [= Reprint from Topoi 3/2, 1993], New Delhi, 1995, pp. 115-146, 2 maps.

Kuwait

1251 C. ROUECHE & S.M. SHERWIN-WHITE, Some aspects of the Seleucid Empire: the Greek inscriptions from Failaka in the Arabian Gulf, *in* Chiron 15, München, 1985, pp. 1-39, 3 Pl.

1252 O. CALLOT, Trouvailles monétaires de Tell Khazneh — Monetary finds at Tell Khazneh, *in* Failaka. Fouilles Françaises 1984-1985 (Y. Calvet & J.-F. Salles, eds.) [= Travaux de la Maison de l'Orient 12], Lyon, 1986, pp. 291-296, fig. 115-116.

1253 R. DALONGEVILLE, Observations géomorphologiques — Geomorphological observations, *in* Failaka. Fouilles Françaises 1984-1985 (Y. Calvet & J.-F. Salles, eds.) [= Travaux de la Maison de l'Orient 12], Lyon, 1986, pp. 110-113, fig. 47.

1254 J. GACHET & J.-F. SALLES, Chantier F5: rapport préliminaire 1985 — Preliminary report: 1985 excavations on F5, *in* Failaka. Fouilles Françaises 1984-1985 (Y. Calvet & J.-F. Salles, eds.) [= Travaux de la Maison de l'Orient 12], Lyon, 1986, pp. 297-330, fig. 117-142.

1255 P. LOMBARD, Une coupe à boire en argent et ses accessoires à Tell Khazneh — A silver drinking set at Tell Khazneh, *in* Failaka. Fouilles Françaises 1984-1985 (Y. Calvet & J.-F. Salles, eds.) [= Travaux de la Maison de l'Orient 12], Lyon, 1986, pp. 281-290, fig. 107-114.

1256 J. MARCILLET-JAUBERT, Une inscription grecque de Tell Khazneh — A Greek inscription at Tell Khazneh, *in* Failaka. Fouilles Françaises 1984-1985 (Y. Calvet & J.-F. Salles, eds.) [= Travaux de la Maison de l'Orient 12], Lyon, 1986, pp. 265-267, fig. 98-99.

1257 C. ROBIN, Les "inscriptions" en écriture sud-arabique — "Inscriptions" in South-Arabian script, *in* Failaka. Fouilles Françaises 1984-1985 (Y. Calvet & J.-F. Salles, eds.) [= Travaux de la Maison de l'Orient 12], Lyon, 1986, pp. 269-272, fig. 100-103.

1258 J.-F. SALLES, Petits objets de Tell Khazneh — Small finds at Tell Khazneh, *in* Failaka. Fouilles Françaises 1984-1985 (Y. Calvet & J.-F. Salles, eds.) [= Travaux de la Maison de l'Orient 12], Lyon, 1986, pp. 245-263, fig. 90-97.

1259 J.-F. SALLES, La céramique de Tell Khazneh — Tell Khazneh: the pottery, *in* Failaka. Fouilles Françaises 1984-1985 (Y. Calvet & J.-F. Salles, eds.) [= Travaux de la Maison de l'Orient 12], Lyon, 1986, pp. 201-244, fig. 77-89.

1260 J.-F. SALLES, Tell Khazneh: les figurines en terre cuite — Terracotta figurines at Tell Khazneh, *in* Failaka. Fouilles Françaises 1984-1985 (Y. Calvet & J.-F. Salles, eds.) [= Travaux de la Maison de l'Orient 12], Lyon, 1986, pp. 143-200, fig. 59-76.

1261 M. SZNYCER, Une inscription araméenne de Tell Khazneh — An Aramaic inscription at Tell Khazneh, *in* Failaka. Fouilles Françaises 1984-1985 (Y. Calvet & J.-F. Salles, eds.) [= Travaux de la Maison de l'Orient 12], Lyon, 1986, pp. 273-280, fig. 104-106.

1262 O. CALLOT, J. GACHET & J.-F. SALLES, Some Notes about Hellenistic Failaka, *in* Proceedings of the Seminar for Arabian Studies 17 [= Proceedings of the 20th Seminar for Arabian Studies 1986], 1987, pp. 37-51, 9 fig.

1263 M. AMANDRY & O. CALLOT, Le Trésor de Failaka 1984 (Koweit), *in* Revue numismatique XXX, 1988, pp. 64-74, Pl. XII-XIV.

1264 V.A. GAIBOV, G.A. KOSHELENKO & S.V. NOVIKIV, Issledovanie pamjatnikov ellinisticeskogo vremeni na ostrove Fajlaka (L' étude de sites d' époque hellénistique dans l' île de Faylaka, *in* Vestnik Drevnei Istorii 185, 1988, n°. 2, pp. 183-201 (with French summary).

1265 F. PIEJKO, The Inscriptions of Icarus-Failaka, *in* Classica et Mediaevalia, Revue Danoise de Philologie et d'Histoire XXXIX, Copenhague, 1988, pp. 89-116.

1266 O. CALLOT, Failaka à l'époque hellénistique, *in* L'Arabie préislamique et son environnement historique et culturel [= Actes du Colloque de Strasbourg, 24–27 juin 1987 (T. Fahd, ed.)], Leiden, 1989, pp. 127-143, 6 fig.

1267 J.B. CONNELLY, Votive Offerings from Hellenistic Failaka: Evidence for Heracles Cult, *in* L'Arabie préislamique et son environnement historique et culturel [= Actes du Colloque de Strasbourg, 24–27 juin 1987 (T. Fahd, ed.)], Leiden, 1989, pp. 145-158, 28 fig.

1268 K. JEPPESEN, The sacred enclosure in the Early Hellenistic Period. With an appendix on epigraphical finds, Danish Archaeological Investigations on Failaka, Kuwait. Ikaros. The Hellenistic Settlements 3 [= Jutland Archaeological Society Publications XVI:3], Copenhagen, 1989, 125 p., 110 fig.

1269 G.J.R. MAAT, H.A. LONNEE & H.J.W. NOORDHUIZEN, Osteology of human skeletons of the Hellenistic Period from Failaka Island, Kuwait, *in* Advances in Paleopathology (L. Capasso, ed.), Chieti, 1989, pp. 135-142.

1270 J. TEIXIDOR, A propos d'une inscription araméenne de Failaka, *in* L'Arabie préislamique et son environnement historique et culturel [= Actes du Colloque de Strasbourg, 24–27 juin 1987 (T. Fahd, ed.)], Leiden, 1989, pp. 169-171, 1 fig.

1271 V. BERNARD, J. GACHET & J.-F. SALLES, Apostilles en marge de la céramique des états IV et V, *in* Failaka. Fouilles françaises 1986-1988 (Y. Calvet & J. Gachet, eds.) [= Travaux de la Maison de l'Orient 18], Lyon, 1990, pp. 241-284, 19 fig.

1272 O. CALLOT, Trouvailles monétaires de l'état IV, Annexe 1, *in* J. Gachet, Un habitat du IIe siècle av. J.-C. dans la forteresse de Failaka, *in* Failaka.

Fouilles françaises 1986-1988 (Y. Calvet & J. Gachet, eds.) [= Travaux de la Maison de l'Orient 18], Lyon, 1990, p. 192.

1273 M.-J. CHAVANE, Petits objets de la forteresse, *in* Failaka. Fouilles françaises 1986-1988 (Y. Calvet & J. Gachet, eds.) [= Travaux de la Maison de l'Orient 18], Lyon, 1990, pp. 285-302, 15 fig.

1274 J.B. CONNELLY, The terracotta figurines. Greek types and cult, *in* Failaka. Fouilles françaises 1986-1988 (Y. Calvet & J. Gachet, eds.) [= Travaux de la Maison de l'Orient 18], Lyon, 1990, pp. 209-220, 2 fig.

1275 J.B. CONNELLY, Hellenistic Terracottas of Cyprus and Kuwait, *in* The Coroplast's Art. Greek Terracottas of the Hellenistic World (J.P. Uhlenbrock, ed.), College Art Gallery & Aristide D., New York, 1990, pp. 94-101.

1276 J. GACHET, Un habitat du IIe siècle av. J.-C. dans la forteresse de Failaka, *in* Failaka. Fouilles françaises 1986-1988 (Y. Calvet & J. Gachet, eds.) [= Travaux de la Maison de l'Orient 18], Lyon, 1990, pp. 167-208, 30 fig., 24 Tab., Dépl. III.

1277 J. GACHET & J.-F. SALLES, Iconographie et cultes à Failaka, Koweit, *in* Mesopotamia XXV, 1990, pp. 193-216, fig. A-B, fig. 53-56.

1278 K. JEPPESEN, Zur Ergänzung, Bestimmung und Datierung der Monumentalbauten des hellenistischen Tempelbezirks auf der Insel Ikaros im persichen Meerbusen, *in* Akten des XIII. Internationalen Kongresses für klassische Archäologie, Berlin, 24–30 Juli 1988, 1990, p. 205.

1279 G.J.R. MAAT, H.A. LONNEE & H.J.W. NOORDHUIZEN, Analysis of human skeletons from the Hellenistic Period buried at a ruined Bronze Age building on Failaka, Kuwait, *in* Failaka. Fouilles Françaises 1986-1988 (Y. Calvet & J. Gachet, eds.), [= Travaux de la Maison de l'Orient 18], Lyon, 1990, pp. 85-102, 8 fig., 4 Tab.

1280 G.J.R. MAAT & M.S. BAIG, Scanning Electron Microscopy of Fossilized Sickle-Cells, *in* International Journal of Anthropology 5/3, 1990, pp. 271-276, 5 fig.

1281 G.J.R. MAAT & M.S. BAIG, Fossilized Human Blood Cells from a Hellenistic Settlement, *in* International Journal of Anthropology 5/3, 1990, pp. 277-280, 4 fig.

1282 J. MARCILLET-JAUBERT, Une nouvelle inscription grecque à Failaka, Annexe 2, *in* J. Gachet, Un habitat du IIe siècle av. J.-C. dans la forteresse de Failaka, *in* Failaka. Fouilles françaises 1986-1988 (Y. Calvet & J. Gachet, eds.) [= Travaux de la Maison de l'Orient 18], Lyon, 1990, pp. 193-195, 1 fig.

1283 J.-F. SALLES, Questioning the BI-ware, *in* Failaka. Fouilles françaises 1986-1988 (Y. Calvet & J. Gachet, eds.) [= Travaux de la Maison de l'Orient 18], Lyon, 1990, pp. 303-334, 10 fig.

1284 R.D. BARNETT, A Plaque from Failaka, *in* Persica XIV, 1990-92, pp. 135-138, 3 fig.

1285 V. BERNARD & J.-F. SALLES, Discovery of a Christian Church at al-Qusur, Failaka (Kuwait), *in* Proceedings of the Seminar for Arabian Studies 21 [= Proceedings of the 24th Seminar for Arabian Studies, held at Oxford on 24th–26th July 1990], 1991, pp. 7-21, 11 fig.

1286 V. BERNARD, O. CALLOT & J.-F. SALLES, L'église d'al-Qousour Failaka, Etat de Koweit. Rapport préliminaire sur une première campagne de fouilles, 1989, *in* Arabian archaeology and epigraphy 2/3, 1991, pp. 145-181, 20 fig.

1287 O. CALLOT, La Forteresse hellénistique de Failaka, *in* Golf–Archäologie. Mesopotamien, Iran, Kuwait, Bahrain, Vereinigte Arabische Emirate und Oman (K. Schippmann, A. Herling & J.-F. Salles, eds.) [= Internationale Archäologie 6, Buch am Erlbach], Göttingen & Lyon, 1991, pp. 121-132, 7 fig.

1288 J. GACHET & J.-F. SALLES, Nouvelles remarques sur la céramique hellénistique de Failaka, *in* Golf–Archäologie. Mesopotamien, Iran, Kuwait, Bahrain, Vereinigte Arabische Emirate und Oman (K. Schippmann, A. Herling & J.-F. Salles, eds.) [= Internationale Archäologie 6, Buch am Erlbach], Göttingen & Lyon, 1991, pp. 145-158, 5 fig.

1289 D. KENNET, Excavations at the site of al-Qusur, Failaka, Kuwait, *in* Proceedings of the Seminar for Arabian Studies 21 [= Proceedings of the 24th Seminar for Arabian Studies, held at Oxford on 24th–26th July 1990], 1991, pp. 97-111, 6 fig.

1290 O. CALLOT, Failaka-Ikaros sous Antiochos III: étude numismatique, *in* Arabia Antiqua. Hellenistic Centres around Arabia [= Serie Orientale Roma 70, II (A. Invernizzi & J.-F. Salles, eds.)], Roma, 1993, pp. 257-273, 12 fig.

1291 J. GACHET & J.-F. SALLES, Failaka, Koweit, *in* Materialien zur Archäologie der Seleukiden- und Partherzeit im südlichen Babylonien und im Golfgebiet (U. Finkbeiner, ed.) [= Ergebnisse der Symposien 1987 und 1989 in Blaubeuren (Deutsches Archäologisches Institut, Abteilung Baghdad)], Tübingen, 1993, pp. 59-85, 13 fig.

1292 J.-F. SALLES, Hellénisme et traditions orientales à Failaka, *in* Arabia Antiqua. Hellenistic Centres around Arabia [= Serie Orientale Roma 70, II (A. Invernizzi & J.-F. Salles, eds.)], Roma, 1993, pp. 223-255.

1293 L. HANNESTAD, The chronology of the hellenistic fortress (F5) on Failaka, *in* Topoi 4/2, 1994, pp. 587-595.

Northeastern Arabia

1294 T. FAHD, Gerrhéens et Gurhumites. Les Gurhumites de la Mekke venaient-ils de Gherra? *in* Studien zur Geschichte und Kultur des Vorderen

Orients [= Festschrift für Bertold Spuler zum siebzigsten Geburtstag (R. Roemer & A. North, eds.)], Leiden, 1981, pp. 67-78.

1295 D.T. Potts, Archaeological perspectives on the Historical Geography of the Arabian Peninsula, *in* Münsterische Beiträge zur antiken Handelsgeschichte II/2, 1983, pp. 113-124, 1 map.

1296 Anonymus, A Linguistic, Tribal and Onomastical Study of the Hasaean Inscriptions, *in* Atlal 8, 1984, pp. 86-108, Pl. 85-90.

1297 M.S. Gazdar, D.T. Potts & A. Livingstone, Excavations at Thaj, *in* Atlal 8, 1984, pp. 55-85, Pl. 60-84.

1298 M. Golding, Artefacts from Later Pre-Islamic Occupation in Eastern Arabia, *in* Atlal 8, 1984, pp. 165-174, Pl. 131-144.

1299 D.T. Potts, Northeastern Arabia. From the Seleucids to the Earliest Caliphs, *in* Expedition 26/3, 1984, pp. 21-30, 12 fig.

1300 J. Ryckmans, Alphabets, Scripts and Languages in Pre-Islamic Arabian Epigraphical Evidence, *in* Pre-Islamic Arabia. Studies in the History of Arabia II [= Proceedings of the Second International Symposium on Studies in the History of Arabia, 1399/1979], Riyadh, 1984, pp. 73-86.

1301 K.M. Eskoubi & S.R.A. al-Aila, Thaj Excavations, Second Seasons 1404/1984, *in* Atlal 9, 1985, pp. 41-53, Pl. 30-49.

1302 J. Ryckmans, A three generations' matrilineal genealogy in a Hasaean inscription: matrilineal ancestry in Pre-Islamic Arabia, *in* Bahrain through the ages, the Archaeology (Shaikha Haya Ali al-Khalifa & M. Rice, eds.), London, 1986, pp. 407-417.

1303 P. Lombard, The Salt Mine Site and the "Hasaean" Period in Northeastern Arabia, *in* Araby the Blest. Studies in Arabian Archaeology (D.T. Potts, ed.), Margaret Golding in Memoriam [= Carsten Niebuhr Institute Publications 7], Copenhagen, 1988, pp. 116-135, 13 fig.

1304 D.T. Potts, Trans-Arabian Routes of the pre-islamic period, *in* L'Arabie et ses mers bordières I: Itinéraires et voisinages (J.-F. Salles, ed.) [= Travaux de la Maison de l' Orient 16], Lyon, 1988, pp. 127-162, 1 fig.

1305 D.T. Potts, Pre-Alexandrine Phoenician staters from northeastern Arabia, *in* Arabian archaeology and epigraphy 2/1, 1991, pp. 24-30, 10 fig.

1306 D.T. Potts, Nabataean finds from Thaj and Qatif, *in* Arabian archaeology and epigraphy 2/2, 1991, pp. 138-144, 7 fig.

1307 A. al-Mughanam, Sassanid dirhams from the island of Tarut, *in* Bahrain through the ages. The History (Sheikha Abdullah bin Khaled & M. Rice, eds.), London, 1993, pp. 409-422.

1308 D.T. Potts, The Sequence and Chronology of Thaj, *in* Materialien zur Archäologie der Seleukiden- und Partherzeit im südlichen Babylonien und im Golfgebiet (U. Finkbeiner, ed.) [= Ergebnisse der Symposien 1987 und

1989 in Blaubeuren (Deutsches Archäologisches Institut, Abteilung Baghdad)], Tübingen, 1993, pp. 88-110, 22 fig., Pl. 1-3a.

1309 D.T. POTTS, The Sequence and Chronology of Ayn Jawan, *in* Materialien zur Archäologie der Seleukiden- und Partherzeit im südlichen Babylonien und im Golfgebiet (U. Finkbeiner, ed.) [= Ergebnisse der Symposien 1987 und 1989 in Blaubeuren (Deutsches Archäologisches Institut, Abteilung Baghdad)], Tübingen, 1993, pp. 111-126, 13 fig., Pl. 3b-3c.

1310 D.T. POTTS, A Sasanian Lead Horse from Northeastern Arabia, *in* Iranica Antiqua XXVIII, 1993, pp. 193-199, 5 fig.

1311 J.A. LANGFELDT, Recently discovered early Christian monuments in Northeastern Arabia, *in* Arabian archaeology and epigraphy 5/1, 1994, pp. 32-60, 24 fig.

1312 D.T. POTTS, Nestorian Crosses from Jabal Berri, in Arabian archaeology and epigraphy 5/1, 1994, pp. 61-65, 9 fig.

1313 D.T. POTTS, Pre-Islamic Coinage in the Eastern Province of Saudi Arabia, *in* Arts & The Islamic World 25 [= Special Volume: Saudi Arabia. Architecture, Archaeology and the Arts], 1994, pp. 41-43, 4 fig.

1314 D.T. POTTS & J. CRIBB, Sasanian and Arab-Sasanian Coins from Eastern Arabia, *in* Iranica Antiqua XXX [= Festschrift K. Schippmann II], 1995, pp. 123-139, 29 ill., 3 Tab.

Bahrain

1315 M. SZNYCER, L'inscription araméenne sur un vase inscrit du Musée de Bahrain, *in* Syria LXI/1-2, 1984, pp. 109-118, 3 fig.

1316 M. KERVRAN, Qal'at al-Bahrain: a strategic position from the Hellenistic period to modern times, *in* Dilmun 12, 1984-'85, pp. 25-31, 3 fig.

1317 D.T. POTTS, Awal and Muharraq, *in* Dilmun 13, 1985-'86, pp. 17-27.

1318 R. BOUCHARLAT, Some notes about Qal'at al-Bahrain during the Hellenistic period, *in* Bahrain through the ages, the Archaeology (Shaikha Haya Ali al-Khalifa & M. Rice, eds.), London, 1986, pp. 435-444, fig. 148-151.

1319 G.W. BOWERSOCK, Tylos and Tyre: Bahrain in the Graeco-Roman World, *in* Bahrain through the ages, the Archaeology (Shaikha Haya Ali al-Khalifa & M. Rice, eds.), London, 1986, pp. 399-406.

1320 M. KERVRAN, Qal'at al-Bahrain: a strategic position from the Hellenistic period until modern times, *in* Bahrain through the ages, the Archaeology (Shaikha Haya Ali al-Khalifa & M. Rice, eds.), London, 1986, pp. 462-469, fig. 159-161.

1321 P. Lombard, Iron Age Dilmun: a reconsideration of City IV at Qal'at al-Bahrain, *in* Bahrain through the ages, the Archaeology (Shaikha Haya Ali al-Khalifa & M. Rice, eds.), London, 1986, pp. 225-232, fig. 63-67.

1322 D. Oates, Dilmun and the Late Assyrian Empire, *in* Bahrain through the ages, the Archaeology (Shaikha Haya Ali al-Khalifa & M. Rice, eds.), London, 1986, pp. 428-434.

1323 J.-F. Salles, The Janussan necropolis and late first millennium B.C. burial customs in Bahrain, *in* Bahrain through the ages, the Archaeology (Shaikha Haya Ali al-Khalifa & M. Rice, eds.), London, 1986, pp. 445-461, fig. 152-158.

1324 M. Kervran, P. Mortensen & F. Hiebert, The Occupational Enigma of Bahrain between the 13th and the 8th Century B.C., *in* Paléorient 13/1, 1987, pp. 77-93, 10 fig., 1 Tab.

1325 M. Kervran, P. Mortensen & F. Hiebert, The Occupational Enigma of Bahrain between the 13th and the 8th Century B.C., *in* Dilmun 14, 1987-'88, pp. 13-38, 10 fig., 1 Pl., 1 Tab.

1326 S. Dalley, Bronzeworking in Dilmun and S. Babylonia, *in* Neo-Assyrian Textual Evidence for Bronzeworking Centres, *in* Bronzeworking Centres of Western Asia (c. 1000–539 B.C.) (J. Curtis, ed.), London, 1988, pp. 102-103.

1327 R. Boucharlat & J.-F. Salles, The Tylos Period (300 BC.–600 AD.), *in* Bahrain National Museum. Archaeological Collections I. A Selection of Pre-Islamic Antiquities from Excavations 1954-1975 (P. Lombard & M. Kervran, eds.), Manama, 1989, pp. 81-131, fig. 151-241.

1328 P. Lombard, The Late Dilmun Period (1000–400 BC.), *in* Bahrain National Museum. Archaeological Collections I. A Selection of Pre-Islamic Antiquities from Excavations 1954-1975 (P. Lombard & M. Kervran, eds.), Manama, 1989, pp. 49-80, fig. 87-150.

1329 P. Lombard, Qal'at al-Bahrain (janvier/mars et novembre/décembre 1989), *in* The Arabian Gulf Gazetteer I,1 (E.C.L. During Caspers, ed.), Leiden, 1990, pp. 11-12, 1 fig.

1330 J. Marcillet-Jaubert, Stèle funéraire du Musée de Bahrein, *in* Syria LXVII/3-4, 1990, pp. 665-673, 4 fig.

1331 Anonymus, Deutsche Archäologen suchen nach Hellenengräbern in Bahrein, *in* Antike Welt 24/1, 1993, p. 80.

1332 A. Herling & J.-F. Salles, Hellenistic Cemeteries in Bahrain, *in* Materialien zur Archäologie der Seleukiden- und Partherzeit im südlichen Babylonien und im Golfgebiet (U. Finkbeiner, ed.) [= Ergebnisse der Symposien 1987 und 1989 in Blaubeuren (Deutsches Archäologisches Institut, Abteilung Baghdad)], Tübingen, 1993, pp. 161-182, 8 fig., Pl. 5-7a.

1333 P. LOMBARD & M. KERVRAN, Les Niveaux "hellénistiques" du Tell de Qal'at al-Bahrain. Données préliminaires, *in* Materialien zur Archäologie der Seleukiden- und Partherzeit im südlichen Babylonien und im Golfgebiet (U. Finkbeiner, ed.) [= Ergebnisse der Symposien 1987 und 1989 in Blaubeuren (Deutsches Archäologisches Institut, Abteilung Baghdad)], Tübingen, 1993, pp. 127-160, 20 fig., Pl. 4.

1334 O. CALLOT, Un trésor de monnaies d'argent et monnaies diverses, *in* F. Højlund & H.H. Andersen, Qala'at al-Bahrain, Vol. 1, The Northern City Wall and the Islamic Fortress. The Carlsberg Foundation's Gulf Project (P. Mortensen, ed.) [= Jutland Archaeological Society Publications XXX:1], Aarhus, 1994, pp. 351-358, fig. 1759-1762.

1335 O. CALLOT, Deux monnaies seleucides trouvées à Qala'at al-Bahrain, *in* F. Højlund & H.H. Andersen, Qala'at al-Bahrain, Vol. 1, The Northern City Wall and the Islamic Fortress. The Carlsberg Foundation's Gulf Project (P. Mortensen, ed.) [= Jutland Archaeological Society Publications XXX:1], Aarhus, 1994, pp. 358-360, fig. 1763-1764.

1336 P.-L. GATIER, Un tesson inscrit en grec, *in* F. Højlund & H.H. Andersen, Qala'at al-Bahrain, Vol. 1, The Northern City Wall and the Islamic Fortress. The Carlsberg Foundation's Gulf Project (P. Mortensen, ed.) [= Jutland Archaeological Society Publications XXX:1], Aarhus, 1994, pp. 317-318, fig. 1722.

1337 C.J. SALTER, Analysis of iron smithing slag, *in* F. Højlund & H.H. Andersen, Qala'at al-Bahrain, Vol. 1, The Northern City Wall and the Islamic Fortress. The Carlsberg Foundation's Gulf Project (P. Mortensen, ed.) [= Jutland Archaeological Society Publications XXX:1], Aarhus, 1994, pp. 382-385, fig. 1881-1892.

United Arab Emirates

1338 R. BOUCHARLAT, Documents arabes provenant des sites "hellénistiques" de la Péninsule d'Oman, *in* L'Arabie préislamique et son environnement historique et culturel [= Actes du Colloque de Strasbourg, 24–27 juin 1987 (T. Fahd, ed.)], Leiden, 1989, pp. 109-126, 8 fig.

1339 M. MOUTON, Les pointes de flèches en fer des sites préislamiques de Mleiha et ed-Dur, E.A.U., *in* Arabian archaeology and epigraphy 1/2-3, 1990, pp. 88-103, 6 fig., 9 Tab.

1340 B. SENIOR, An Important Dated Coin from the Arabian Peninsula, *in* Newsletter n°. 132 of the Oriental Numismatic Society, February-April 1992, 1 p., 1 fig.

1341 E. HAERINCK, Héraclès dans l'iconographie des monnaies arabes préislamiques d'Arabie du Sud-est?, *in* Akkadica 89-90, 1994, pp. 9-13, 10 fig.

1342 O. CALLOT, Arabian coins from the Sharjah Museum, *in* Tribulus. Bulletin of the Emirates Natural History Group 5/1, 1995, p. 26.

Abu Dhabi

1343 R. BOUCHARLAT &. P. GARCZYNSKI, First Survey at Hili 14, *in* R. Boucharlat & P. Lombard, The Oasis of Al Ain in the Iron Age: Excavations at Rumeilah 1981-1983. Survey at Hili 14, *in* Archaeology in the United Arab Emirates IV, 1985, pp. 62-64, Pl. 67-70.

1344 R. BOUCHARLAT & P. LOMBARD, The Oasis of Al Ain in the Iron Age: Excavations at Rumailah 1981-1983. Survey at Hili 14, *in* Archaeology in the United Arab Emirates IV, 1985, pp. 44-73, Pl. 35-73.

1345 R. BOUCHARLAT & P. LOMBARD, Datations absolues de Rumeilah et chronologie de l'Age du Fer dans la péninsule d'Oman, *in* Golf–Archäologie. Mesopotamien, Iran, Kuwait, Bahrain, Vereinigte Arabische Emirate und Oman (K. Schippmann, A. Herling & J.-F. Salles, eds.) [= Internationale Archäologie 6, Buch am Erlbach], Göttingen & Lyon, 1991, pp. 301-314, 2 fig., 4 Tab.

1346 K.G. STEVENS, Four "Iron Age" stamp seals from Qarn bint Sa'ud (Abu Dhabi Emirate — U.A.E.), *in* Arabian archaeology and epigraphy 3/3, 1991, pp. 173-176, 5 fig.

1347 G.R.D. KING & P. HELLYER, A Pre-Islamic Christian site on Sir Bani Yas, *in* Tribulus. Bulletin of the Emirates Natural History Group 4/2, 1994, pp. 5-7, 1 ill.

1348 K.G. STEVENS, Surface finds from Qarn bint Sa'ud (Abu Dhabi Emirate — U.A.E.), *in* Mesopotamia XXIX, 1994, pp. 199-262, 25 fig.

Sharjah

1349 M. MOUTON, The Historical Periods: The Soundings, *in* II. The Sharjah Coast, *in* 2nd Archaeological Survey in the Sharjah Emirate, 1985 — A Preliminary Report (N.H. al-Abboudi & R. Boucharlat, eds.), Sharjah & Lyon, 1989, pp. 20-25, fig. 11-23, Pl. V-IX.

1350 R. BOUCHARLAT, Note on an Iron Age hill settlement in the Jabal Buhais, *in* Archaeological Surveys and Excavations in the Sharjah Emirate, 1990 and 1992. A Sixth Interim Report (R. Boucharlat, ed.), Lyon, 1992, p. 20, fig. 1 & 33.

1351 R. BOUCHARLAT & A. PECONTAL-LAMBERT, The 1990 excavations at Jabal Buhais, an Iron Age cemetery, *in* Archaeological Surveys and Excavations in the Sharjah Emirate, 1990 and 1992. A Sixth Interim Report (R. Boucharlat, ed.), Lyon, 1992, pp. 11-18, fig. 5-9 & 30-32.

1352 A. BENOIST & M. MOUTON, L'Age du Fer dans la Plaine d'al-Madam (Sharjah, EAU): Prospection et fouilles récentes, *in* Proceedings of the Seminar for Arabian Studies 24 [= Proceedings of the 27th Seminar for Arabian Studies held in London on 22–24 July 1993], 1994, pp. 1-12, 4 fig.

1353 A. BENOIST & M. MOUTON, Archaeological Investigations in the al-Madam Area, *in* Archaeological Surveys and Excavations in the Sharjah Emirate, 1993 and 1994. A Seventh Interim Report (M. Mouton, ed.), Lyon & Sharjah, 1994, pp. 43-46, fig., Pl.

1354 R. DALONGEVILLE, Physical Presentation of the Region of al-Madam, *in* Archaeological Surveys and Excavations in the Sharjah Emirate, 1993 and 1994. A Seventh Interim Report (M. Mouton, ed.), Lyon & Sharjah, 1994, pp. 39-42, fig., Pl.

1355 J.M. CORDOBA & M. MOUTON, La cultura del hierro en la peninsula de Oman. Excavaciones hispano-francesas en el emirato de Sharjah, *in* Revista de Arqueologia XVI — 169, Mayo 1995, pp. 16-25, ill.

Mleiha

1356 A. HESSE, Electromagnetic Survey on Mleiha Site, *in* 2nd Archaeological Survey in the Sharjah Emirate, 1985 — A Preliminary Report (N. H. al-Abboudi & R. Boucharlat, eds.), Sharjah & Lyon, 1989, p. 37, fig. 32-33, Pl. XVI.

1357 R. BOUCHARLAT & M. MOUTON, Excavations at Mleiha Site: A Preliminary Report, *in* Archaeological Surveys and Excavations in the Sharjah Emirate, 1986. A Third Preliminary Report (N.H. al-Abboudi, ed.), Department of Culture & Information, Sharjah, 1990, pp. 38-50, fig. 11, 18-37, Pl. VII-XIII.

1358 A. BOUCHER & A. HESSE, Geophysical Surveys in Mleiha Area, *in* Archaeological Surveys and Excavations in the Sharjah Emirate, 1986. A Third Preliminary Report (N.H. al-Abboudi, ed.), Department of Culture & Information, Sharjah, 1990, pp. 26-37, fig. 11-17, Tab. 2-4.

1359 Y. CALVET, A Rhodian Stamped Amphora Handle from Mleiha, 1986, *in* Archaeological Surveys and Excavations in the Sharjah Emirate, 1986. A

Third Preliminary Report (N.H. al-Abboudi, ed.), Department of Culture & Information, Sharjah, 1990, p. 51, fig. 37:4.

1360 C. Robin, Inscriptions from the Mleiha Region, *in* Archaeological Surveys and Excavations in the Sharjah Emirate, 1986. A Third Preliminary Report (N.H. al-Abboudi, ed.), Department of Culture & Information, Sharjah, 1990, p. 52.

1361 T. Mitchell, An Inscription in Epigraphic South-Arabian Script from Sharjah, *in* Persica XIV, 1990-'92, pp. 131-134, ill.

1362 R. Boucharlat, From the Iron Age to the "Hellenistic" period. Some evidence from Mleiha (United Arab Emirates), *in* Golf–Archäologie. Mesopotamien, Iran, Kuwait, Bahrain, Vereinigte Arabische Emirate und Oman (K. Schippmann, A. Herling & J.-F. Salles, eds.) [= Internationale Archäologie 6, Buch am Erlbach], Göttingen & Lyon, 1991, pp. 289-300, 5 fig., 1 Tab.

1363 R. Boucharlat & M. Drieux, Appendix 1. A Note on Coins and a Coin Mold from Mleiha, Emirate of Sharjah, U.A.E., *in* D.T. Potts, The Pre-Islamic Coinage of Eastern Arabia [= Carsten Niebuhr Institute Publications 14], Copenhagen, 1991, pp. 110-117, 9 fig.

1364 R. Boucharlat & M. Mouton, Cultural Change in the Oman Peninsula during the Late 1st Millennium B.C. as seen from Mleiha, Sharjah Emirate (U.A.E.), *in* Proceedings of the Seminar for Arabian Studies 21 [= Proceedings of the 24th Seminar for Arabian Studies, held at Oxford on 24th–26th July 1990], 1991, pp. 23-33, 6 fig.

1365 M. Barbier, The bone objects workshop of the site of Mleiha (Area BV), *in* Archaeological Surveys and Excavations in the Sharjah Emirate, 1990 and 1992. A Sixth Interim Report (R. Boucharlat, ed.), Lyon, 1992, pp. 49-55, fig. 27-29.

1366 A. Gautier, Preliminary report on the fauna of Mleiha, *in* Archaeological Surveys and Excavations in the Sharjah Emirate, 1990 and 1992. A Sixth Interim Report (R. Boucharlat, ed.), Lyon, 1992, pp. 56-57.

1367 S. Kay, An Ancient Past, *in* Sharjah. Heritage & Progress, Dubai, 1992, pp. 74-77, 6 fig.

1368 M. Mouton, K. Mokaddem & P. Garczynski, Excavations at Mleiha, 1990 and 1992 campaigns, *in* Archaeological Surveys and Excavations in the Sharjah Emirate, 1990 and 1992. A Sixth Interim Report (R. Boucharlat, ed.), Lyon, 1992, pp. 21-44, fig. 10-26 & 34-39.

1369 D. Ramadan, Münzgussformen und Festungsreste im Emirat Sharjah entdeckt, *in* Antike Welt 23/4, 1992, p. 320.

1370 J. Teixidor, Une inscription araméenne provenant de l'Emirat de Sharjah (Emirats Arabes Unis), *in* Comptes rendus de l'Académie des Inscriptions

& Belles-Lettres, Séances de l'année 1992 (novembre-décembre), Paris, 1992, pp. 695-707, 3 fig.

1371 R. BOUCHARLAT & M. MOUTON, Mleiha (3e s. avant J.-C.–1er/2e s. après J.-C.), *in* Materialien zur Archäologie der Seleukiden- und Partherzeit im südlichen Babylonien und im Golfgebiet (U. Finkbeiner, ed.) [= Ergebnisse der Symposien 1987 und 1989 in Blaubeuren (Deutsches Archäologisches Institut, Abteilung Baghdad)], Tübingen, 1993, pp. 219-249, 18 fig.

1372 R. DALONGEVILLE & M. MOUTON, French Archaeological Mission in Sharjah — Results of the 1993 Season, *in* Tribulus. Bulletin of the Emirates Natural History Group 3/2, 1993, pp. 14-15, Pl. I on p. 19.

1373 A. BENOIST, K. MOKADDEM & M. MOUTON, Excavations at Mleiha Site. The 1993 and 1994 seasons, *in* Archaeological Surveys and Excavations in the Sharjah Emirate, 1993 and 1994. A Seventh Interim Report (M. Mouton, ed.), Lyon & Sharjah, 1994, pp. 11-19, fig., Pl.

1374 R. BOUCHARLAT & M. MOUTON, Mleiha (Emirate of Sharjah, UAE) at the beginning of the Christian era, *in* Proceedings of the Seminar for Arabian Studies 24 [= Proceedings of the 27th Seminar for Arabian Studies held in London on 22–24 July 1993], 1994, pp. 13-26, 6 fig, II Pl.

1375 O. CALLOT, Mleiha: Local issues of the Arabian pre-islamic coinage, *in* Archaeological Surveys and Excavations in the Sharjah Emirate, 1993 and 1994. A Seventh Interim Report (M. Mouton, ed.), Lyon & Sharjah, 1994, pp. 21-22, Pl.

1376 Y. CALVET, Greek Amphora Stamps from Mleiha (1993), *in* Archaeological Surveys and Excavations in the Sharjah Emirate, 1993 and 1994. A Seventh Interim Report (M. Mouton, ed.), Lyon & Sharjah, 1994, pp. 23-24, Pl.

1377 R. DALONGEVILLE, Mleiha: physical study and palaeo-environment, *in* Archaeological Surveys and Excavations in the Sharjah Emirate, 1993 and 1994. A Seventh Interim Report (M. Mouton, ed.), Lyon & Sharjah, 1994, pp. 7-10, fig. 1-3.

1378 M. MOUTON, Results of the 1994 archaeological season in Mileiha, *in* Tribulus. Bulletin of the Emirates Natural History Group 4/2, 1994, pp. 7-9.

1379 A. PLOQUIN, Early metallurgical activities in Mileiha, *in* Tribulus. Bulletin of the Emirates Natural History Group 4/2, 1994, pp. 9-10.

1380 A. PLOQUIN & S. ORZECHOWSKI, Palaeo-metallurgy at Mleiha: preliminary notes, *in* Archaeological Surveys and Excavations in the Sharjah Emirate, 1993 and 1994. A Seventh Interim Report (M. Mouton, ed.), Lyon & Sharjah, 1994, pp. 25-32, fig., Pl.

1381 A. PRIEUR, Molluscs from Mleiha, *in* Archaeological Surveys and Excavations in the Sharjah Emirate, 1993 and 1994. A Seventh Interim Report (M. Mouton, ed.), Lyon & Sharjah, 1994, pp. 33-38.

1382 M. MOUTON, Fouilles françaises en Arabie orientale. Mleiha (IIe siècle av. J.-C. / IVe siècle ap. J.-C.), *in* Orient Express. Notes et Nouvelles d'Archéologie Orientale, Paris, 1995, n°. 2, pp. 40-43, 2 fig.

1383 A.V. SEDOV, Two South Arabian coins from Mleiha, *in* Arabian archaeology and epigraphy 6/1, 1995, pp. 61-64, 4 fig.

Umm al-Qaiwain

Ed-Dur

1384 R. BOUCHARLAT, E. HAERINCK, C.S. PHILLIPS & D.T. POTTS, Archaeological Reconnaissance at ed-Dur, Umm al-Qaiwain, U.A.E., *in* Akkadica 58, 1988, pp. 1-26, 16 fig., III Pl., 1 map.

1385 R. BOUCHARLAT, E. HAERINCK, O. LECOMTE, D.T. POTTS & K.G. STEVENS, The European Archaeological Expedition to ed-Dur, Umm al-Qaiwayn (U.A.E.). An Interim Report on the 1987 and 1988 Seasons. Introduction, *in* Mesopotamia XXIV, 1989, pp. 5-11, fig. A-B, fig. 1.

1386 E. HAERINCK & K.G. STEVENS, The Belgian Excavations in 1987, *in* The European Archaeological Expedition to ed-Dur, Umm al-Qaiwayn (U.A.E.). An Interim Report on the 1987 and 1988 Seasons, *in* Mesopotamia XXIV, 1989, pp. 57-72, fig. AO-AU, fig. 38-61, Pl. V-VI.

1387 O. LECOMTE, R. BOUCHARLAT & J.-M. CULAS, Les fouilles françaises, *in* The European Archaeological Expedition to ed-Dur, Umm al-Qaiwayn (U.A.E.). An Interim Report on the 1987 and 1988 Seasons, *in* Mesopotamia XXIV, 1989, pp. 29-56, fig. AB-AN, fig. 12-37, Pl. I-IV.

1388 D.T. POTTS, The Danish Excavations, *in* The European Archaeological Expedition to ed-Dur, Umm al-Qaiwayn (U.A.E.). An Interim Report on the 1987 and 1988 Seasons, *in* Mesopotamia XXIV, 1989, pp. 13-27, fig. C-AA, fig. 2-11.

1389 R.L. WHITE, An Analysis of Bitumen from ad-Door, *in* Emirates Natural History Group (Abu Dhabi) Bulletin 38, July 1989, pp. 14-17, 2 fig., 1 Tab.

1390 E. HAERINCK, Archeologische onderzoekingen in de Verenigde Arabische Emiraten, in Tentoonstellingcatalogus Vlaamse Archeologie. Opgravingen in binnen- en buitenland, Oudenburg, 1990, p. 101, 2 fig.

1391 E. HAERINCK, Ed Dur (Umm al Qaiwain, United Arab Emirates) (2nd Season by the Belgian Team), *in* The Arabian Gulf Gazetteer I,1 (E.C.L. During Caspers, ed.), Leiden, 1990, pp. 15-16, 1 fig.

1392 O. LECOMTE, Fouilles Françaises à ed-Dur, Umm al-Qaiwayn, Emirats Arabes Unis, *in* The Arabian Gulf Gazetteer I,1 (E.C.L. During Caspers, ed.), Leiden, 1990, pp. 13-14, 1 fig.

1393 E. Haerinck, C. Metdepenninghen & K.G. Stevens, Excavations at ed-Dur (Umm al-Qaiwain, U.A.E.) — Preliminary report on the second Belgian season (1988), *in* Arabian archaeology and epigraphy 2/1, 1991, pp. 31-60, 43 fig.

1394 P. Hellyer, Winter Excavations at Ad Door, in Tribulus. Bulletin of the Emirates Natural History Group 1/1, 1991, pp. 18-20, 2 fig.

1395 E. Haerinck, C. Metdepenninghen & K.G. Stevens, Excavations at ed-Dur (Umm al-Qaiwain, U.A.E.) — Preliminary report on the third Belgian season (1989), *in* Arabian archaeology and epigraphy 3/1, 1992, pp. 44-60, 23 fig.

1396 E. Haerinck, Excavations at ed-Dur (Umm al-Qaiwain, U.A.E.) — preliminary report on the fourth Belgian season (1990), *in* Arabian archaeology and epigraphy 3/3, 1992, pp. 190-208, 35 fig.

1397 E. Haerinck, Excavations at ed-Dur (Umm al-Qaiwain, U.A.E.) — preliminary report on the fifth Belgian season (1991), *in* Arabian archaeology and epigraphy 4/3, 1993, pp. 210-225, 20 fig.

1398 E. Haerinck, C.S. Phillips, D.T. Potts & K.G. Stevens, Ed-Dur, Umm al-Qaiwain (U.A.E.), *in* Materialien zur Archäologie der Seleukiden- und Partherzeit im südlichen Babylonien und im Golfgebiet (U. Finkbeiner, ed.) [= Ergebnisse der Symposien 1987 und 1989 in Blaubeuren (Deutsches Archäologisches Institut, Abteilung Baghdad)], Tübingen, 1993, pp. 183-193, 5 fig., Pl. 7b.

1399 P. Hellyer, 20,000 graves at Ad Door site, *in* Tribulus. Bulletin of the Emirates Natural History Group 3/1, 1993, p. 24.

1400 O. Lecomte, Ed-Dur, les occupations des 3e et 4e s. ap. J.-C.: Contexte des trouvailles et matériel diagnostique, *in* Materialien zur Archäologie der Seleukiden- und Partherzeit im südlichen Babylonien und im Golfgebiet (U. Finkbeiner, ed.) [= Ergebnisse der Symposien 1987 und 1989 in Blaubeuren (Deutsches Archäologisches Institut, Abteilung Baghdad)], Tübingen, 1993, pp. 195-217, 15 fig.

1401 R.C. Senior, Aghudaka? A new discovery gives a clearer reading, *in* Numismatic Studies 3, New Delhi, 1993, pp. 35-38, 3 fig.

1402 W. Van Neer & A. Gautier, Preliminary report on the faunal remains from the coastal site of ed-Dur, 1st — 4th century A.D. Umm al-Quwain, United Arab Emirates, *in* Archaeozoology of the Near East. Proceedings of the first international symposium on the archaeozoology of southwestern Asia and adjacent areas (H. Buitenhuis & A.T. Clason, eds.), Leiden, 1993, pp. 110-118, 2 fig., 1 Tab.

1403 E. Haerinck, Excavations at ed-Dur (Umm al-Qaiwain, U.A.E.) — Preliminary report on the sixth Belgian season (1992), *in* Arabian archaeology and epigraphy 5/3, 1994, pp. 184-197, 34 fig.

1404 J.K. PAPADOPOULOS, A Western Mediterranean amphora fragment from ed-Dur, *in* Arabian archaeology and epigraphy 5/4, 1994, pp. 276-279, 2 fig.

1405 D.T. POTTS, The diffusion of light by translucent media in antiquity: à propos two alabaster window-pane fragments from ed-Dur (United Arab Emirates), *in* Antiquity 69, 1995, pp. 182-188, 2 fig.

Ras al-Khaimah

1406 C.S. PHILLIPS, Wadi al Qawr, Fashgha 1. The Excavation of a Prehistoric Burial Structure in Ras al-Khaimah, U.A.E., 1986. A Preliminary Report [= Department of Archaeology, University of Edinburgh. Project Paper 7], 1987, 32 p., 39 fig.

1407 D. KENNET, Jazirat al-Hulayla-early Julfar, with a Historial Commentary by G.R.D. King, *in* Journal of the Royal Asiatic Society 4, 1994, pp. 164-212, ill.

Fujairah

1408 P. HELLYER, Iron Age Fort in Fujairah, *in* Tribulus. Bulletin of the Emirates Natural History Group 3/2, 1993, p. 17.

1409 P. HELLYER, Safavid and Sassanian Coins in Fujairah, *in* Tribulus. Bulletin of the Emirates Natural History Group 5/1, 1995, p. 25.

Oman

1410 D.T. POTTS, From Qadê to Mazûn: four notes on Oman, c. 700 B.C. to 700 A.D., *in* The Journal of Oman Studies 8/1, 1985, pp. 81-95.

1411 D.T. POTTS, The Location of Iz-ki-e, *in* Revue d'Assyriologie et d'Archéologie orientale 79, 1985, pp. 75-76.

1412 P.M. COSTA & T.J. WILKINSON, Excavations at 'Arja, *in* The Hinterland of Sohar. Archaeological Surveys and Excavations within the Region of an Omani Seafaring City (P.M. Costa & T.J. Wilkinson, eds.), *in* The Journal of Oman Studies 9, 1987, pp. 133-144, fig. 58-63, Pl. 60-73.

1413 P.M. COSTA & T.J. WILKINSON, Introduction, *in* The Hinterland of Sohar. Archaeological Surveys and Excavations within the Region of an Omani Seafaring City (P.M. Costa & T.J. Wilkinson, eds.), *in* The Journal of Oman Studies 9, 1987, pp. 13-22, 1 fig., 4 Pl.

1414 P.M. COSTA, Pre-Islamic Izki: some field evidence, *in* Proceedings of the Seminar for Arabian Studies 18 [= Proceedings of the 21st Seminar for Arabian Studies 1987], 1988, pp. 15-23, 9 Pl.

1415 G. WEISGERBER, Oman: A Bronze-producing Centre during the 1st Half of the 1st Millennium B.C., *in* Bronze-working Centres of Western Asia c. 1000–539 B.C. (J. Curtis, ed.), London, 1988, pp. 285-294, Pl. 158-170.

1416 P. YULE & G. WEISGERBER, Samad ash Shan. Excavation of the Pre-Islamic Cemeteries. Preliminary Report, Bochum, 1988, 53 p., 11 fig., 16 Pl.

1417 F. DE BLOIS, Maka and Mazun, *in* Studia Iranica 18/2, 1989, pp. 157-167.

1418 J.J. ORCHARD & J.C. ORCHARD, The University of Birmingham Archaeological Expedition to the Sultanate of Oman, *in* The Arabian Gulf Gazetteer I,1 (E.C.L. During Caspers, ed.), Leiden, 1990, pp. 22-24, 2 fig.

1419 P. YULE, Activities of the German Mission to the Sultanate of Oman, 1989, *in* The Arabian Gulf Gazetteer I,1 (E.C.L. During Caspers, ed.), Leiden, 1990, p. 21, 1 fig.

1420 P. YULE & G. WEISGERBER, Samad ash Shan, Sultanate of Oman, 1989 — Abstract, *in* Proceedings of the Seminar for Arabian Studies 20 [= Proceedings of the 23rd Seminar for Arabian Studies, held at London on 18th–20th July 1989], 1990, pp. 141-144, 2 fig.

1421 M.KERVRAN & F. HIEBERT, Sohar pré-islamique. Note stratigraphique, *in* Golf–Archäologie. Mesopotamien, Iran, Kuwait, Bahrain, Vereinigte Arabische Emirate und Oman (K. Schippmann, A. Herling & J.-F. Salles, eds.) [= Internationale Archäologie 6, Buch am Erlbach], Göttingen & Lyon, 1991, pp. 337-348, 8 fig.

1422 P. YULE, Life and the Afterlife. Archaeological Excavations in Wadi Samad, *in* Tribute to Oman 10, 1991, pp. 182-188, fig.

1423 P. YULE & G. WEISGERBER, Excavation of the Late Iron Age cemetries in the Wadi Samad, Sultanate of Oman, 1987 — Summary, *in* Golf–Archäologie. Mesopotamien, Iran, Kuwait, Bahrain, Vereinigte Arabische Emirate und Oman (K. Schippmann, A. Herling & J.-F. Salles, eds.) [= Internationale Archäologie 6, Buch am Erlbach], Göttingen & Lyon, 1991, pp. 331-336.

1424 P. YULE, Samad al Shan. Eine vorislamitische Nekropole im Sultanat Oman, *in* Nürnberger Blätter zur Archäologie 9, 1992-'93, pp. 39-48, Abb. 33-43.

1425 P. YULE, Excavations at Samad al Shan 1987-1991, Summary, *in* Proceedings of the Seminar for Arabian Studies 23 [= Proceedings of the 26th Seminar for Arabian Studies, held at Manchester 1992], 1993, pp. 141-153, 6 fig.

1426 P. YULE & B. KAZENWADEL, Toward a Chronology of the Late Iron Age in the Sultanate of Oman, *in* Materialien zur Archäologie der Seleukiden- und Partherzeit im südlichen Babylonien und im Golfgebiet (U. Finkbeiner, ed.) [= Ergebnisse der Symposien 1987 und 1989 in Blaubeuren (Deutsches Archäologisches Institut, Abteilung Baghdad)], Tübingen, 1993, pp. 251-276, 10 fig.

1427 P. YULE & M. KERVRAN, More than Samad in Oman: Iron Age pottery from Suhar and Khor Rori, *in* Arabian archaeology and epigraphy 4/2, 1993, pp. 69-106, 15 fig.

1428 P. YULE, Grabarchitektur der Eisenzeit im Sultanat Oman, *in* Baghdader Mitteilungen 25, 1994, pp. 519-577, Taf. 18-23, 12 Tab.

INDEX OF AUTHORS

ORIENTALISTE, KLEIN DALENSTRAAT 42, B-3020 HERENT